PARENTING THROUGH THE SEASONS

A Companion for Self-Discovery
and Daily Life with Children

SHERRY JENNINGS

With illustrations by Viorica Jennings

WECAN
WALDORF EARLY CHILDHOOD
ASSOCIATION OF NORTH AMERICA

Parenting Through the Seasons
A Companion for Self-Discovery and Daily Life with Children

First English Edition

© 2025 by Sherry Jennings

Illustrations © 2025 by Viorica Jennings

All rights reserved. No part of this book may be reproduced without the written permission of the publisher, except for brief quotations embodied in critical reviews and articles.

ISBN 978-1-936849-66-6

Published in the United States of America by
    Waldorf Early Childhood Association of North America
    285 Hungry Hollow Road
    Spring Valley, NY 10977
    www.waldorfearlychildhood.org

Visit our online store:
store.waldorfearlychildhood.org

This publication was made possible by a grant from the Waldorf Curriculum Fund.

What will our children do in the morning
if they do not see us fly?
    —Rumi

Table of Contents

About This Book 9
About Me 13

Planting Hope 19

WINTER — EARTH

JANUARY: The Bewitching Hour 25
FEBRUARY: Nesting in New England 31
MARCH: Bursting at the Seams 39

Warmth in the Winter 47

SPRING — WATER

APRIL: Word for the Day: Water 55
MAY: Dancing into the Sun 63
JUNE: A Summer Symphony 71

Summer School for Toddlers 77

SUMMER — AIR

JULY: Wonder and Gratitude 83
AUGUST: Savoring the Last Bites 89
SEPTEMBER: Gathering Abundance 95

Rhythm, Ritual, and the Unexpected 101

AUTUMN — FIRE

OCTOBER: Goodbye and Hello 111
NOVEMBER: Lighting the Way 117
DECEMBER: Peaceful Moments 125

Growing as a Parent and a Person 131

In Gratitude 139
About the Author and Illustrator 141

In order for a thing to speak to you
You must regard it for a certain time
As the only one that exists
And through your laborious and exclusive love
The one and only phenomenon is now placed
    at the center of the universe
And in that incomparable place on that day
It is attended by angels.

    —Rainer Maria Rilke

About This Book

At the beginning of 2023, when I was the Parent and Child Teacher at the High Mowing Waldorf School, I was asked to write a monthly article for the Young Child Blog on the school's newly updated website. After several months of sharing my musings, I realized that I was enjoying the writing process and was receiving positive feedback from community members, both parents and non-parents. I continued writing the monthly articles until June of 2025.

In that month, I retired after fifty years of teaching early childhood classes at the school. What next? Someone once said to me that retiring is not driving away from your professional life and parking the car in the garage. Retiring is *re-tiring*, getting a new set of tires. Where would I go with a new set of tires?

What to do with the pages of writings and musings that resided on my computer? What to do with the experiences and learnings I had gathered? Why not compile it all into a book? A book would be a fun and creative challenge, providing an opportunity for me to share my years of living and teaching with a broader audience. I had a plan for re-tiring. And here it is!

Before you begin

The first section of each chapter describes my **personal experiences in the natural world**, followed by **information on child development** and support for caregivers of young children, and then **activities** to enhance young children's experience of the seasons.

As a reader, you get to choose how you want to approach this book. You may decide to read it from cover to cover. You may choose to go directly to a specific month. Perhaps you are interested specifically in one of the three elements. For example, the aspect of experiencing nature may be of interest, so you could focus on the first several paragraphs. If parenting support and child development are your interests, head to the middle paragraphs. If it is a stormy day in March and you feel like screaming, first scream, but not at your children, then turn to the final section of the March entry, where there may be a "life-saving" suggestion for what to do with your lovely, lively children that stormy day.

After each section you will find an essay which contributes to enlarging the picture of that season.

As you delve into the book, it will become clear that I live in New England, the northeastern corner of the United States. My nature experiences come out of living in a four-season climate in the Northern Hemisphere. If you live in the south or the west, you will have a different orientation to the natural world and your journey through the year will look very different from mine.

Though the ways in which nature expresses itself and the ways you relate to each season depend on your geographic location, the forces and elements of nature will be the same. The birth of spring may be a long, slow, cheery whistle in

New England, while in the South, it may be a short, jubilant shout. Enjoy finding the experience of each month wherever you are!

Families come in all forms, shapes, and constellations. In the text I have used the terms "parent" and "caregiver" interchangeably when referring to adults who care for children.

You may want to stop reading now if you are looking for a "How-To" book. You will find no footnotes or bibliography, referring to articles and research papers that elucidate the content or prove my point. The words here flow out of my connection with the natural world, my experiences as a teacher, and as a parent. They flow out of who I am as a person. All I can offer to reassure you is to say I have tried my best to be an honest observer and an accurate reporter of myself and the world.

About Me

I grew up as an only child in a rural setting with parents who loved me. I spent many happy hours outside on my swing in an old apple tree, watching the patterns of the sun and trying to pump high enough to touch the leaves. I made cakes in my sandbox, gathered eggs with my grandmother across the road, swung on grapevines, and went for walks in the forest with my parents. Oh, those quiet summer afternoons lying on my back enclosed in my private space, a clump of young quaking aspens, reading a good book, and watching the twirling leaves dance overhead. Other days, it was off to explore in the dump of an old abandoned farmhouse for "valuables."

I remember the smell of the woods in October as we gathered black walnuts and dug sassafras root for tea. I remember looking at the stars on cold winter nights and pondering the Universe. I remember standing in an unexpected, warm spring rain wearing only underpants. I remember the summer afternoons with my cousins, hurling tiny white berries at each other before heading sweaty and red-faced to the pump on the back porch of my grandparents' house, where we drank the coldest water I have ever tasted before collapsing on the grass holding our aching bellies. I still wonder what happened to the shoebox that I kept in a secret place in my bedroom, the one that held my treasures—a dried snakeskin, special stones and pieces of wood, and a cow's tooth I had found in a nearby pasture.

Looking back, I realize that those childhood experiences in the world outside had a profound influence on who I am today. I love being outside, walking in the woods, and gardening. I am fascinated by the forms and colors I find outside. I have learned about expansion and contraction by observing the development of leaves in plants. I have explored how water flows as I trench run-off away from my walkway. I have an insatiable curiosity about how nature works. I find peace as I walk through the forest, and sometimes I am gifted with new and exciting ideas. Some I have even incorporated into this book. When I step outside, wonder is waiting.

I have found nature to be a friend, teacher, comforter, sustainer, and provider. Nature restores and refreshes. She is beauty and truth. The medical field is only now catching up to what humans have known for many years: nature is a healer. She helps to alleviate stress, lower blood pressure, relieve headaches, reduce pain, improve breathing, and temper depression. Being outside in nature can soothe your soul and lift your spirit. Some physicians are even writing scripts for patients that prescribe one-half hour of daily time in the woods. Being in nature is a multi-faceted self-care experience!

About being a parent, what can I say? I have loved every moment of it, even the challenging ones. Through the years, I have felt excited, overwhelmed, exhausted, joyful, frightened, sad, hopeful, and loved. I have stretched and grown. If you are deep in the trenches at the moment, you may be feeling exhausted and overwhelmed. Don't worry, the joy will return.

As a teacher, I was dedicated to providing children in my classrooms with opportunities to experience the wonder and beauty of nature firsthand. We walked the same path through the forest every day, marveling at the changes that had occurred. We gathered the treasures the earth has to offer to take to our classroom. No classroom can ever have too many acorns and pine cones! They become trees in a puppet show, loaves of bread, bowls of apples or potatoes, bales of hay! We planted flowers, caught frogs, and, in addition, strengthened arms and legs as we hopped over stones and balanced on logs. We made it a practice to go outside every day unless there was a deluge or the temperature was lower than ten degrees Fahrenheit.

As I begin to articulate the foundation on which I stand, I realize that rather than standing with my two feet firmly planted on the ground, I stand with my feet firmly planted in two streams. Fifty years ago, I signed up for a six-week eurythmy course, having no idea what eurythmy is, knowing only that it involved moving my body. There, I became aware of Rudolf Steiner's writings. Rudolf Steiner (1861-1925) was an Austrian philosopher, architect, educator, economic reformer, scientist, and artist. His writings are based on a picture of the human being as a being composed of body, soul, and spirit. I recognized immediately that I had landed. Never mind moving my body, I had found a home for my soul and spirit. Within weeks, I was on my way to becoming a Waldorf teacher. I had stepped into the stream of anthroposophy and Waldorf education, and I continue to find strength, nourishment, and guidance in that stream.

Over twenty years ago, I sat in a faculty meeting and heard an individual speak about Nonviolent Communication. Nonviolent Communication (NVC) or Compassionate

Communication was developed by Marshall Rosenberg (1934-2015) in the 1980s, stemming from his work with Carl Rogers and individuals with mental illnesses. I immediately saw a direction for exploring my interest in human relationships, as well as the possibility of gathering tools for effective communication, even in conflicts. In half an hour of listening, I realized I had landed again. Within a few weeks, I signed up for a Nine-Day Intensive Training Course designed specifically for individuals with an understanding of and experience with NVC. Even though I had no prior understanding or experience, just a feeling that this was for me, I enrolled in the course and have remained a student of NVC ever since. Through this work with NVC, I have gained new insights about myself and developed my capacity to express myself honestly and compassionately. I have gained skills to support me in social situations that call for conflict resolution, mediation, and speaking the truth in challenging interactions. I stand firmly in the stream of Nonviolent Communication.

I have thoroughly enjoyed the process of writing this book. It has enabled me to consolidate my thoughts, refine my writing skills, and collaborate with a team of professionals. I have been delighted by the creativity that evolved as I sat for many hours at my computer. In the process, I have experienced and expressed qualities I value having in my life—authenticity, honesty, respect, being heard and seen.

I have experienced joy, but I have also experienced times of fear and doubt. Can I do this? Is the writing good enough? Will anybody read it? Should I rewrite portions? There is no time for rewrites now!

It is autumn now in New England. The light is receding and the darkest time of the year is approaching. It takes courage to go into the dark, whether outer or inner. At the same time the light has a clarity unlike any other time of the year and there is a crispness in the air. I feel infused with a new energy. It is a time for celebrating the power and courage of human beings to overcome doubt and fear, to heal and transform themselves and the world. I can find within myself the courage to meet fear and doubt, so I will now send the final portion of the manuscript off to the editors.

Putting together this book has led me on an unexpected and amazing journey. It has been a gift that I will be unwrapping many times over. Reader, I hope this offering will, in turn, be a gift to you. I hope you find at least one tiny treasure to tuck into a pocket for your journey as a parent and as a person.

With warmth and respect for your journey,

—Sherry Jennings

Planting Hope

I planted my sweet peas early this year—a sunny day just before the cool April rains set in again. Roundish, hard seeds, rolling off my fingers into the dark, moist soil. Sweet peas love the cool, moist earth before the days grow hot. If the earth dries out, the seeds will not be happy. In fact, I usually soak them overnight so they will germinate in 10 to 14 days, but this year I forgot. When I looked this morning—on day 14—there was no sign of a sprout, but I am not worried yet.

I remember that morning when I was loosening the cool soil with my fingers to make a home for the seeds, seeds that had come from blossoms and, hopefully, to blossoms would return. I was not only planting the seeds with their tough outer coat. I was planting thin, fragile stems with their delightful, curly, whimsical tendrils reaching out to find an anchor. I was planting pastel silk and the sweet fragrance of the bouquets my mother would bring inside from her garden. I was planting delicate softness, sweet smells, beauty, and the warmth of summer days. I was planting hard kernels of hope.

In these turbulent times, this is what we, as caregivers and teachers, need to plant for our children: kernels of hope. How can we do this? By having hope ourselves. Children are sensitive beings who resonate with the feelings and thoughts of the adults around them. They drink in what is present in their parents' inner lives, for better or worse. Whether it is the expletive that comes after the hammer hits the thumb, the content of a phone call relaying sad news, or the joyful announcement of a newly born cousin, very young children take these emotions into their beings even though they are too young to understand and process them.

As grown-ups, we may be overwhelmed and distraught when we read the news or contemplate the many issues facing humanity today—climate change, war, immigration, and world hunger. However, it is important to set these issues aside when we are with our young children and offer thoughts and feelings that are filled with hope and positivity. They do not yet need explanations of what is going on in the outer world or awareness of our fears and concerns. We need to meet the children with optimism and hope. There will be plenty of time later for them to come face to face with the darker sides of what may be happening in the world.

The same offering gesture holds true for Goodness, Truth, and Beauty. We want the young child who is just beginning to get to know the world to experience that the world is a wonderful place, a place filled with Goodness, Truth, and Beauty. If young children are surrounded with love and positivity, they will experience that the world in which they have been born is good.

What does this look like?

All the warmth, love, affection, and tenderness you surround them with tells them the world is a good place.

The warm clothing, nourishing food, beauty, and order in their homes tell them the world is a good place.

Connections with neighbors, cousins, grandparents, and other relatives and friends tell them the world is good.

Being outside and drinking in the cheery good morning of the cardinals, the fragrance of the lilacs, the darting dance of dragonflies, the parade of tiny ants tells them the world is good.

Don't forget all the treasures waiting to be collected—acorns, pine cones, seashells, and the amazing selection of rocks. All of these tell the children that the world is a wonderful, magical, good place to be.

Seeking colors and forms in nature, in art, in music, offers goodness and beauty.

Leave the world news and political discussions until after they are in bed. Even if they are not yet able to understand, they are affected by the mood and conversations of the adults around them.

Whenever possible, give them the opportunity to grow annual flowers. Planting seeds, watching them sprout and turn into flowers, watching the flowers grow and wither, and then discovering one day that there are seeds again, provides an outer picture of the quality of Hope. This picture is something the young child can internalize.

Look for kernels of hope wherever you go! And plant some yourselves.

WINTER —

EARTH

from *Winter Trees*

>A liquid moon
>moves gently among
>the long branches.
>Thus having prepared their buds
>against a sure winter
>the wise trees
>stand sleeping in the cold.
>
>—William Carlos Williams

JANUARY

The Bewitching Hour

I sit looking out the window of my studio. The ferns are bronze, the earth brown, the trees bare. My soul longs for a gentle snowfall, just enough to cover the ground, but not enough that I need to shovel. I want it to make a soft blanket over the brown earth, covering up the trowel that I never retrieved in November, the one that is hiding somewhere among the perennials I never got around to cutting back. I know the snow will simplify the landscape and help me hold on to the peace I felt in the last days of December.

Already in the first days of January, the pace of life is picking up as I return to my tasks in this new year. I have used all the holiday leftovers from my freezer; I need to take up cooking again. My young adult children who piled in for the holidays have gone; now I need to wash all the sheets and restore order. Then there are thank you notes, unanswered phone calls, the unfinished writing project, and school preparations. I long for that blanket of snow so that when I look out my window, I see peace and tranquility.

As parents of young children, you may also be feeling an onslaught of projects and tasks. The children's interest in their toys has waned, and they are whining or squabbling among themselves. It is too cold to just open the door and let them run outside; layers of warmth are required for comfort and safety. Then there is the never-ending production of meals and clean laundry.

Perhaps you eventually find a quiet moment before sleep and say to yourself, "I need to change something. I resolve to no longer use a loud voice to get my children's attention." After all, it is January, the time for making resolutions.

As for me, I no longer make New Year's resolutions. By the third day of January, I would have forgotten to exercise, by the fifth, I would not have written in my journal for three days, and even at the end of seven days, I would still be eating too much chocolate. By the fifteenth day I might have forgotten what my resolutions were. I have finally realized what preordained failure looks like. Now I slide delicately into the New Year.

Before I can decide what I want to ask of myself, I need to know who is advising me, as many voices echo in my brain. Is it the one who wants me to eat less sugar? Is it the one who wants me to finish making clothes for the naked dolls I made two years ago? Is it the one who wants me to make my morning meditation time longer? Is it the one who shouts, "Don't be so lazy! Get on with writing that memoir." If I had listened to all of them, I would have collapsed in a heap, maybe not even gotten out of bed. As I moved through the early days of January, some voices faded, and some I asked to be quiet. Now I was ready to find a cozy blanket, sit by the wood stove, and listen to my own voice. I find it is actually more possible and more fun that way. By starting with my intentions on the fifth or sixth or tenth day of January, I have already removed the pressure of a perfect year.

Here in New England the cold weather is conducive to slowing down, to nesting, to contemplation. The quiet mood of winter has moved in and invites me to look ahead. Now I can consider my intentions for the new year.

I want to be realistic, so I request only two actions of myself as I enter the months ahead: one for my body, one for my soul and spirit. This year, I chose to work on improving my balance and to read from an inspirational text for at least ten minutes every morning.

After many years of "falling short," I have finally come up with a method that works for me. Here is my strategy for approaching New Year's resolutions:

> 1. I clarify why I am making the resolution. The WHY is important because it clarifies the positive that I am seeking. Then, I choose a realistic action I can take that would support me in making this change.
>
> 2. I make a specific request of myself, including a realistic time frame, not the whole year. For example, "I will do yoga for 20 minutes on Mondays, Wednesdays, and Fridays for a month," not "I will exercise more this year." I find that if I make the request very specific, I am more likely to do what I am asking of myself.
>
> I have also found that if I frame my intention as a request rather than as a demand, I am more likely to follow through. When I view my intentions as requests, I actually consider how I am served by fulfilling the request. What do I long for? What do I value? What will

I enjoy more if I am actually able to make this change? I am free to choose what I actually want to do. When I see my intentions as demands I impose on myself, I put unnecessary pressure on myself to perform to a particular standard. Then if I fall short, I feel bad and judge myself harshly. "Oh, you blew it again." Yet, if I am relaxed and make a request, my chances of actually following through are greater.

3. At the end of the month, I check to see if I have fulfilled my request; I am accountable only to myself. "Of the 12 times I intended to do yoga, I actually did it 9 times."

4. When I tally up, I am kind and gentle with myself. I remind myself that it is not the perfection, but the essence of the intention and the striving that are important to me. I can try again.

5. Forward Ho!

Now you may wonder how this can help you with parenting. First, remember tiny steps may get you to your destination faster, as you won't fall over so easily. For example, perhaps you say to yourself:

I would like more peace at dinner so we can share a conversation.

For the next two weeks, on Mondays and Wednesdays, I will prepare enough food to last for two days. I will then be more relaxed, and the likelihood of starting the meal in a quiet mood will increase.

On the second Thursday, I will assess how many times I succeeded and if my strategy supported peaceful meal conversations.

I managed only three of the four times, but on those "Leftover Days," there was peace at the table. Good try!

Forward Ho! I will try it again for two more weeks.

Peace during the "Bewitching Hour"

As you consider your resolutions, you might want to address the hour before dinner, known as the Bewitching Hour. The baby is crying, and the toddler is hungry, tired, and cranky. You are tired and hungry, trying not to be cranky as you realize you don't remember whether you ate lunch. Once in my early days of parenting three young children, my mother came for a visit. I saw her in the kitchen at 9:00 am, and I wondered why she was making dinner. I soon figured it out. If dinner was prepared at 9:00 am, the hour from 4:00 to 5:00 pm was more peaceful.

Here are some suggestions for the Bewitching Hour at your house if dinner is in the oven.

• Put everyone under the age of five into a warm bath.

• Make some Play Dough. The warmth in the children's hands will be soothing.

>Bluebell Play Dough
>***not edible***
>
>3 cups flour
>¾ cup salt
>3 teaspoons cream of tartar
>3 cups water
>3 tablespoons oil
>1 ½ tablespoons vanilla extract
>2 drops lavender oil

Combine dry ingredients in a saucepan. Add water and oil and whisk until smooth. Cook over medium heat until nearly set.

Add vanilla and lavender, stir until well blended.

Remove from the saucepan from the heat and knead until the dough cools. If you wish to color the dough, add food coloring or watercolor paint to the desired tint.

Stores well and needs no refrigeration if kept in an airtight container.

- Leave the laundry unfolded and take out a book for everyone to enjoy.

- In the kitchen, have a drawer or basket dedicated to toys or games that are only brought out during the Bewitching Hour.

- If you are still finishing dinner preparations, find a way to involve your child in the process. Get out the carrots. For the preschooler, there are metal crinkle cutters shaped like a cleaver with a wooden handle. With one hand on top and the other on the handle, your child can safely cut carrot coins for dinner. For safety, cut the carrot in half lengthwise so it doesn't roll when your child begins cutting.

- Get out the carrot and carrot peeler. I did this with my youngest, an energetic four-year-old, and he was content. He would peel and peel until only a matchstick-sized carrot remained, but, in the meantime, I had chopped the salad.

Even though it is mid-January, it is not too late! You can make a new resolution at any moment!

Just remember: Keep it *simple* and *specific*!

FEBRUARY

Nesting in New England

Winter has gotten off to a slow start in New England this year. Although there have been many very cold nights, measurable snow has only recently fallen, and now there have been three storms in one week. Suddenly, a whole new world of activities opens up. There is sledding, snowshoeing, skiing, and for the grown-ups, there is snow shoveling.

There is a beauty of looking out into a pure white, snow-covered vista. Uncompleted garden tasks are buried. Rather than being a reminder of work undone, the uncut, dried flower heads of the perennials delight as they dance in the wind, revealing the beauty of their dried geometry and providing lunch for the birds. Thankfully, toys and tools left scattered in the yard won't appear until the snow has melted to reveal autumn's unfinished tasks.

The world outside is literally black and white; the white surface spreads across the land, cut through by the black of tree trunks and limbs. Only the pines dare to hold out against this two-color vista. The complex images of colorful flowers, foliage of many shades of green, rocks and stones of all sizes, shapes, colors, textures, which offered us a sensory feast in the summer, are buried beneath a blanket of white. This winter landscape is simple and easy to take in. It asks little of us but to enjoy and stay safe.

In summer, our attention was focused outward. The world around us was alive with waltzing flowers, buzzing bees, and the songs of birds. Our souls reached for the sun, for family and friends, for expanding and exploring the endless wonders of nature.

Now the days are shorter; the warmth of the sun recedes. In the quiet of the black and white landscapes and long, quiet evenings, our souls turn inward. We are given the opportunity to ponder, to reflect. "Who am I?" "What are my next steps as a person?" "As a parent?" When I first asked these questions, in addition to "Who am I?" there was also "WHAT do I want to be when I grow up?" Now the question has become "WHO do I want to be when I grow up?" Our souls yearn to stretch and grow, to take up new tasks, whether they be in the world around us or in our own inner growth, our own transforming. Whether we are parents or not, the inwardness and quiet of winter offer the possibility to consider these questions.

Yes, winter in New England is a time to hunker down, contemplate, and assess any questions or situations that need attention. At the same time, winter offers moments to take up activities for which there wasn't time as we worked, gardened, took vacations, or spent our days outside with our children. Now could be the time to read an exciting book, take an armchair vacation, or perhaps sort out the overflowing recipe folder, clean out the everything drawer, sort out a closet, or just do nothing for a little while. That is allowed. Daydreaming is a necessary part of life.

However, at times, the cold and dark can seem oppressive. Most of us don't live in cabins anymore, but cabin fever can be a reality in New England in February, especially in a week with three storms. Whether delightful or disappointing, the holiday memories have dimmed, the late February swelling of the tree buds has not yet happened, and it is cold! Perhaps you live in a small space, maybe your five- and six-year-olds are challenging your patience as they bounce off the sofa and coffee tables while swirling capes and brandishing swords. Then there are the layers and layers of clothing that you have to peel back in order to do a simple diaper change. Going outside? NO WAY!

You might even say to yourself, "I sure could use a breath of fresh air and so could the children." Then the reality of putting snow pants, jacket, scarf, hat, and boots on a squirming toddler creeps in. Never mind having to navigate tiny hands into tiny mittens that will immediately be pulled off. Judgments then arise about the person who designed the snowsuits and winter gear in the first place. Clearly not a caregiver of young children!

Now hot and sweaty, you are unable to remember whether you had lunch or even breakfast. You may even decide to scrap the entire expedition. It is just too much!

Reminding yourself you both need fresh air, you take charge, forge ahead anticipating the delightful rush of cold air filling your lungs as you step outside. Later, refreshed by a walk, snowman, sled ride, snow angel, or catching snowflakes on your tongue, you are ready to take up the reverse process—removing all the layers you so carefully applied earlier. This may be followed by "Let's take a nap!"

If you are a new parent and are thinking of looking for sales on winter gear for next year, look for the ones with the longest zippers and fewest snaps. With well-designed gear you may be surprised how even a two-year-old can participate in getting dressed to go outside.

For the children, the snow offers fun and play once they are dressed in all the layers and it isn't dangerously cold. Even a three-year-old can be out in ten-degree weather for a few minutes. A bit of fresh air can soothe a weary soul whether adult or child, deflate conflicts, and relieve stress. Marveling at the perfection in just one tiny snowflake can release tension and offer new perspectives. The fresh air can deliver a burst of energy to take up the tasks yet to come. The extra energy needed to get everyone outside may be worth it.

You and your little ones

What about days that are too cold for the little ones, one child is bouncing off the walls and the other has a fever, or you are not able to muster the forces to go through the dressing and undressing processes? What to do in those moments when cabin fever hits?

• Take out a book you have never shared with your child and enjoy the pictures and stories.

• Crawl on the floor with your child while playing hide and seek/peek-a-boo.

• Find a soft cloth or silk and let it gently flutter down over your child while singing about snow. Don't panic! Put any words you make up to some tune you already know, like "Hot Cross Buns" or "Snow Falls Down" — or enjoy the silence of the moment.

• Fill a sink with warm, soapy water and some measuring spoons and plastic cups. Add an egg beater and your child can make pies and muffins. I found Ivory liquid makes excellent bubbles. This is also a good activity in the bathtub. When tensions or sibling conflicts arise, fill the tub with warm water, give the children some bubble bath and an old-fashioned egg beater and watch them make foam cakes and whipped bubble cookies.

• Mix flour and water dough for kneading. Maybe add a small rolling pin. It doesn't have to be edible. It is about the activity; it is the process, the doing, not the product.

• Feast your eyes on the colorful flowers pictured in the newly arrived seed catalogs while you and your child enjoy the bright colors

• For older toddlers take a large-eyed needle, thick yarn, and a piece of burlap or old knitted sweater. You thread the needle, double the thread, make a knot, and see what they make. You need not teach them anything, just let them stitch. In the end they may tell you what they have made — a dog, a dolly, or banana.

• Bake or cook with your child something for dinner or to share with a neighbor.

• Provide your child with a spray bottle of plain water, a soft cloth and a window.

• Take a nap together.

- Learn a new nursery rhyme or two, make up gestures to illustrate, and repeat over and over and over. Especially with infants, rhymes in which you actually touch the child are connecting and offer possibilities for learning body geography. Remember if they find a rhyme they like, they will want it over and over and over and over. Young children find repetition soothing and fun. There is the anticipation for what comes next and then it comes.

- Sing or put on some music and dance with your child.

- Try anything that can elicit a giggle! Stand on your head, bend over and look at your child through your legs, put a potholder on your head while spinning in a circle, dance with a wooden spoon.

> The sun came up this morning
> *(make a circle with arms overhead)*
>
> and chased the stars away
> *(release circle while fluttering fingers)*
>
> and kissed my Poppet on the nose
> *(touch pointer finger gently on child's nose)*
>
> with a How-do-you-do-today.
>
> —from *Catch Me & Kiss Me & Say It Again* by Clyde Watson (Philomel Books, 1978)

These are a few suggestions. Be creative! Anything new, adventuresome, novel. An occasional change in the usual rhythm may alleviate cabin fever.

Suggestions for you

Don't forget *you!*

During naptime, read a novel and leave the laundry unfolded.

Find a way to get out of the house and take a walk without your child.

Squeeze in a long soaking bath if you can manage. Epsom salts add an extra boost of healing for the body, and with a few drops of essential oil added soothing for the soul.

Even if you do not find a way to do any of these things, stop and breathe and imagine that you are doing them.

Remember, spring is on its way!

MARCH

Bursting at the Seams

March came in like a lamb this year, then quickly transformed into a lion with howling northwest winds. Whether or not these winds have blown winter away, only time will tell. Yes, the weather is unpredictable, despite what the weather forecasters tell us. We only have to use our eyes to see what is really happening. In my yard, I have discovered tulips up two inches, maples budding, and birds singing again. Soon, tiny shoots will begin to appear, offering snowdrops and crocuses.

All winter, seeds have been sleeping under the snow, listening to the whispers of the stars, receiving a message for their growth in the spring and summer ahead. As the days lengthen, the warming earth encourages the seeds to poke through the soil. They reach and stretch until the sprouting seeds burst out of their jackets.

When you begin to unpack last year's spring and summer clothes, you may find that your children are also bursting out of their jackets. Their little bodies have been hidden under many warm layers. Now that they are popping out, you can see how much they have grown since last fall. What fit them just a few months ago is now too short, too tight, too small.

In March, everything begins to turn. The clocks turn, the seasons turn, the leaves turn and twirl in the March winds, the sun turns northward. In New England, human beings turn their thoughts from cold and snow and keeping the fire burning to opening windows, springtime hikes, and planting flowers. It is a time of turning from inside to outside, of turning the focus away from the contemplative, introspective days of winter and looking toward days of sunshine, walking by a rushing stream, watching the grass awaken blade by blade. Snowdrop, crocus, daffodil, and dandelion, the earth begins to turn to life, to growth, and we want to witness the changes.

Young children are also turning away from spending many hours inside during the cold winter months; they are ready to burst out of the house. They are turning towards exploration, excitement, and freedom. Freedom from snowsuits, hats, boots, mittens; from being enclosed within the four walls of their homes. What joy to go outside unencumbered by clothing or freezing temperatures! What joy to feel the squishy mud in boots or between toes! What joy to run freely to investigate what is behind the next bush. And what joy to go as slowly as they want!

Yes, spring is in the air, and the children can sense it. They are ready for excitement, adventure, and exploration. They are longing for the freedom to run, jump, and twirl, to discover what their bodies can do. You can take advantage of the transition time between winter and summer to explore the new and burgeoning world outside with them.

No bugs, and lots of sunshine and warm, gentle breezes, offering nourishment for the senses and the soul.

As you move outside with your young children this spring, they will move with varied paces. Sometimes racing, sometimes spending endless minutes to ponder a tiny pebble or inspect every dandelion—all 98 of them. You can enjoy those moments, not explaining, merely pondering with your child, contemplating the wonder of it all, while you give them the space and time to observe, touch, and enjoy, you can also experience the gifts of nature yourself. Let the wonder of the world sink into your soul, as well as your children's.

On springtime walks with your children, enjoy the worms, bugs, and blossoms with them. Know that you are offering them not only an experience of nature but also the opportunity to build the capacity for a quality essential to the human soul—gratitude for what we have been given. Young children, before the age of seven, learn mainly through imitation. Like a sponge, they absorb what they experience around them, both through their senses and through the inner moods and attitudes of the adults around them. As young children, they are open and imitative, not just of what you do but also of what is going on inside you. If you are joyful and grateful for the wonders of spring, they will be joyful and grateful also.

During walks in nature, especially in springtime, when the changes are visible day to day, the children also take in the process of transformation—not with their intellect but with their eyes. They will see this process in the outside world. Still, the picture will live inside their souls for the future when they begin to experience transformation in themselves—first in the clothes they have outgrown, in the height lines that creep up the kitchen wall, in their bodies in puberty, then as teenagers when their minds expand with knowledge, and later as adults when their souls evolve and transform as they meet the experiences of their lives. Your children will have pictures and images to ground them.

So early spring walks are not just for exercise and letting off steam. They are for helping to establish a foundation for your child's future with the building blocks of wonder, gratitude, and a sense of the power of transformation.

Slowly meander through your yard, a park, or nearby forest as you and your child discover each new shoot, bud, or tiny bug. Take time to welcome each new sign of spring. You need not offer any scientific information on growing processes or photosynthesis. Rather, "Oh, Crocus, I am so happy to see you again." Your children will find many new, exciting things to capture their attention. If you find something special you would like them to see, you can merely point or say "Oh!" You need only stand quietly and marvel at the mystery of the world. Your child will sense the joy, wonder, reverence, and gratitude in your soul and resonate with it.

Frequently walking the same path every day enables the child to see how things change and grow. They will observe how big the new leaves have grown in just a few days or maybe even overnight. They will see, over time, the buds open and the leaves appear. Change happens right before their eyes. These meandering walks in nature will offer you, as well as your children, beauty, health, joy, and a sense of connection as you experience the world together. You will also be offering your child the opportunity to observe transformation as it occurs, as what was a tight bud becomes a colorful blossom. The children will carry within them a picture of the Earth changing and growing. This image of transformation can offer them strength for their futures, as they grow into adulthood. What a gift for a lifetime!

You will soon see robins have returned, juncos and finches are flitting in pairs, and chickadees fly with bits of moss and fluff to line nests. Spring is literally in the air! The delightful songs of the winged ones have called forth the first flowers—snowdrops, crocuses, hellebores—which peek out from beneath brown leaves. These first blossoms are undaunted by frosty nights, cold rain, or even sleet and snow. They may shrivel and wilt, only to arise again when the warm sun appears.

How like one-year-olds learning to walk! They stand up, fall down, stand up, fall down, stand up, until they are upright, and then begin to move on their own across the floor and the lawn. Suddenly, there can be a moment when they plant their feet firmly, raise their arms to the sky, and say without words, "Look at me!" Unconsciously, they recognize they are now upright human beings just like their parents. They are no longer like the animals crawling over the earth on all fours. They have become human, standing upright with hands free to make, to do, to fully explore the world. As adults the memory of that moment is buried deep within our unconscious, but if we could recover it, I can only imagine the tingling delight.

And what delight the children can experience now that spring has arrived. Unencumbered by layers and layers of clothing, the door opens and out they go. There is a new world to explore for beginning walkers, toddlers, and runners. Stones, sticks, dried leaves, soggy acorns are picked up with hands newly set free. Mud puddles call to be stomped and stirred with sticks. The earth is alive with possibility! As a young kindergarten child said to me as we were taking our daily walk through the forest, "This is real Spring!"

As parents, your hearts may yearn to explore and experience the parade of new life, new growth. After winter, you may also be longing to experience nature's rebirth outside. How wonderful to share the joy and hope of spring with your child!

Spring Activities

• Put on your puddle boots and splash in the puddles with them.

• Visit a farm and watch the spring lambs frolic and the peeps following their mothers around the farmyard.

• As you walk, share your excitement: "Oh, look what I see!"

• Kneel down on the warming earth, separate the dried leaves, and together discover tiny shoots and new leaves. Say, "Thank you Mother Earth!"

• Take hands, dance, and sing, "Hello, Spring! Hello, Spring! What beautiful treasures you bring."

• Have the first picnic of the year—a blanket, a basket with lunch just outside your door. Maybe then lie back on the blanket and watch the clouds roll by as you soak up some long-awaited sunshine.

• Go to a pond and look for pollywogs.

• Enjoy all the movements bodies can make now that the earth is firm and bodies are no longer encumbered with heavy clothing.

- Encourage the children to roll down hills, walk on downed logs, jump in puddles, and hop over stones. These activities develop a healthy body awareness, which the children need in order to learn to read and write.

- Find a swing! Swinging is great fun and an important activity that helps to develop bodily capacities for learning once they are in school.

- Put aside your fears and concerns, whether personal or for the world. You can pick them up later if you want.

- Be in the moment. Allow Earth's reawakening to stir hope, joy, and goodness in your soul. Without a word spoken, your children will also come to feel the goodness of being on the earth. This sense of goodness will live on in your children and be a source of strength when, as teens and young adults, they encounter challenging experiences.

The world is at your doorstep. Walk out and enjoy spring with your children!

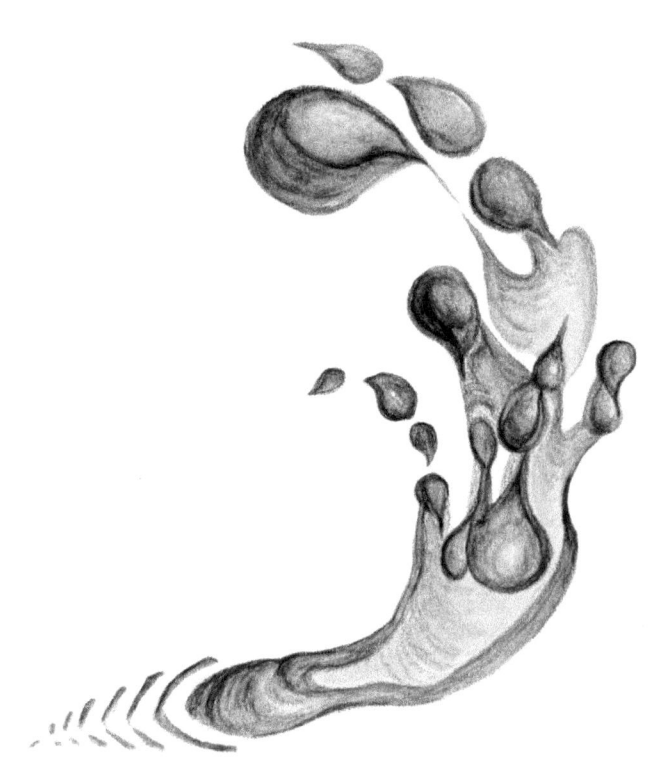

Warmth in Winter

Why keep your child warm?

Physical warmth is an essential element for the healthy growth and development of the human being; a need which if not met can lead to illness, stunted growth, and even a lack of capacity to develop social skills.

For its life processes the human has the same needs as the plant kingdom—air, light, water, nutrition, and a specific amount of warmth.

Imagine for a moment that you are a gardener with a tiny, delicate seedling in your care. Spring is only just beginning and the days are still quite cool. In order to protect the seed from frost and to encourage it to grow, you first put it into a heated greenhouse. There, the concentration of the sun's rays provides the warmth which the sprout needs to continue its growth. Only later when the stem is sturdy and the first sets of leaves well-formed to catch the sunlight and the air temperature outside has warmed do you put the plant outside.

In its physical growth, the young child is like a plant. A seedling needs a specific amount of sunlight and warmth to develop and become a strong pepper or pumpkin plant. The young child needs a specific amount of warmth to grow properly.

This warmth serves several functions in the growing organism:

• to keep the body alive and functioning

• to maintain a specific temperature inside the body to provide for the development of the inner organs—liver, kidneys, heart, and lungs, and so on

• to enable the body to grow and increase in size

• to keep the skin temperature warm enough so that the child feels like moving, socializing, and reaching out into the environment

When a healthy baby is born, all systems are in place; however, they are not fully developed. Only during the first seven years and beyond, does the body complete its physical development and growth. In order to stay alive and grow, young children have at their disposal the calories of heat provided by the nourishment in the food ingested. How much of this energy is needed to keep the organism alive and how much is available for growth is determined by the food and clothing as well as the individual nature of the child.

If the energy and warmth provided by the caregivers are adequate, the child will stay warm and comfortable and the internal organs will have all of the heat they need to grow and mature. However, if the warmth provided is not adequate to serve all of these needs, one or more of these processes will be "short-changed." The most basic need of the human body is to stay alive, so the first warmth available will go into keeping the organism alive. Second, the available warmth will go into the forming and growth of the vital inner organs.

A New England mother described to me her child's early months. He was born in June and gained weight until his third month, and then stopped gaining and even began to lose weight by the fourth month. She then took up her doctor's suggestion that she put woolen underwear on him. Within three weeks her son had gained more weight than he had in the previous three months. When this same mother began to put layers of wool on her older child, her daughter ceased having colds, coughs, and a dripping nose.

In addition to the effects of insufficient warmth on growth and development of the organs and systems of the body, if a child is not sufficiently warm enough, she will not feel as expansive and open to moving either physically or socially. When the physical, survival needs have been met and the child feels warm and comfortable, there will be more likelihood that the child will reach out into her surroundings and connect with others. For example, an infant who is not warm enough will not engage in active movement of the limbs; self-preservation kicks in and the organism prohibits movement in order to preserve resources. In this scenario the development of muscle tone, coordination, and physical strength and the natural overcoming of certain developmental reflexes may be affected. In play, she may not engage as readily with caregivers or other children.

As a teacher, I once observed an amazing overnight transformation in this realm. A child in my class stayed by himself most every day during outside play time in the winter and wandered about the playground. One day I spoke to the mother and requested that she put a woolen sweater on him under his winter jacket. The next day the parents honored my request and added a woolen sweater and warmer hat and mittens to the child's attire. That very day the child began to engage in social, interactive play with his friends, rolling in the snow, laughing, and running.

Another mother sought support from me when she became pregnant with her second child and her two-year-old had never slept through the night, often waking three or four times. She was feeling very concerned, wondering how she would get enough sleep and survive once the second child was born. It so happened that the handout that day was an article on warmth and the growing child. The next week when she returned to the Parent and Child Class, she was so excited. She had gone home the previous week, read the article and put more clothes and blankets on the child before she put him to bed. Lo and behold! He slept through the night, as he did every night thereafter.

Warmth is also connected with the healing processes in the human body. During certain illnesses fever stimulates the immune system to greater activity against germs. Fevers that are monitored and not allowed to get too high are actually healing. If the fever is not suppressed, the warmth will help to literally burn out the illness. Sometimes, if a fever does not materialize during the initial stages of a cold, a hot bath followed by dressing warmly and bedrest will help the cold progress and move out of the body. Warmth also brings relaxation and a sense of ease.

How to keep your child warm

Although there is the impulse to keep the infant or young child toasty warm, children's own sense of temperature is not fully developed until approximately age nine, and they are dependent on their caregivers to judge for them. While the parent, like the child, is replacing old cells, maintaining the body, and at times healing, the parent is no longer developing the inner organs or needing to add body mass or weight. In addition, parents usually spend far less time outside than their child does. Yet adults often judge how warm to dress their child by how warmly they themselves are dressed.

So how can a parent or caregiver know if a child is warm enough, especially since the young child needs to be kept warmer than adults? One easy way is to feel the child's hands. If the hands or feet are cold, the child needs to have on more clothing. Fingers, toes, and skin on all parts of the body will feel warm to the touch if the child is warm enough so that all areas where warmth is needed are receiving the heat that they need. Often adding one more layer to your child's attire than you have on will do the trick.

What does this look like practically? In the cold winter months, a general rule of thumb is three layers on the top and two on the bottom. On the top, this could be long underwear—wool if possible, a turtleneck, and a wool sweater; on the bottom, long johns—wool if possible and heavy pants or overalls. Then it's jacket, snow pants, hat, mittens, wool socks, and warm boots for going outside. Of course, common sense is needed here, depending on how warm it is inside the house or what the outside temperature conditions are. If the child is sweating and the face is red, remove a layer. If the child still has cold hands, try a hat even if the child is playing inside.

With adequate attire and warmth, children can grow healthy, strong bodies and have fun at the same time!

SPRING —

WATER

The beautiful spring came; and when Nature resumes
Her loveliness, the human soul is apt to revive also.
—Harriet Ann Jacobs

APRIL

Word for the Day: Water

The snows of March have disappeared, melting into the sun-warmed earth and streams. In April, Mother Nature displays her wondrous beauty in the outer world moment by moment. The maple flowers explode like fireworks, carpeting the ground with tiny magenta stars. The soft gray buds of the pussy willow plump themselves up until they are just the right size for a ladybug's pillow. The delicate purple chalices of the crocus collect the early morning dew as daffodils trumpet the day and tulips display their bright garments. Soon, the green rosettes of dandelions will raise up miniature suns to greet the day as myriads of green shapes are sprinkled overhead, leafing the world.

Venturing further afield reveals the wonders of the forest. Sharp eyes will be rewarded with the sight of tiny colt's foot suns, violets, vinca, lady slippers, and the fragrant trailing arbutus. What a beautiful world to introduce to your young children! What a beautiful world that can nourish your soul with color and sound!

Suddenly, you feel a new burst of energy. Spring Cleaning Time! Washing windows, getting out the summer clothes, passing along those that no longer fit, and vacuuming the dusty cobwebs from the ceiling. Then, when you can no longer stay inside, you go out into the world. This time, maybe even to begin to reclaim the earth around you. Perhaps raking away the leaves, planting some pansies, and preparing a garden bed. These are all activities in which you can involve your young child. They, too, will take delight in digging in the earth, raking the leaves, and exclaiming at the tiny green shoots popping up. As they look for puddles to splash in and streams to dam, they will hear the birds singing forth the flowers.

As you take up your spring tasks—washing windows or raking leaves—invite your children to join you in the work. Actually, you probably won't even need to invite them, as young children want to do what we do. Just start raking and they will be at your side. Young children learn through imitation. They also want to use tools that are like yours. Small imitation tools—often plastic and breakable—are unsatisfying and usually don't work. (The exception is small plastic leaf rakes, which work quite well.) There is a truth in your tools that is not present in the plastic ones. Your tools actually do the job and hopefully are made to last. Offer your child real tools that are actually effective in taking on the task at hand. Most come in small sizes or you can improvise—cut off handles, or give them a long-handled trowel instead of a spade, for example. And remember to enjoy what you are doing! Your child will drink in your inner mood of joy as well as how carefully you treat the tiny seedlings. And why not sing while you work?

If it is at all possible, start some seeds with them—something they can later transplant outside or direct sow. If no outside garden space is available, try parsley or basil, which you can keep on a windowsill. If this all seems too much to you as parents of young children, perhaps a neighbor or grandparent loves to garden.

Remember, as caregivers of young children, you are very busy and don't have to do it all. Caring for young children is a big task and a huge responsibility; we need all the help we can get. Don't be afraid to ask for help. As my mother always said to me, "Don't be afraid to ask. The worst they can say is NO." Be gentle and patient with yourself. Whatever experiences of new growth, new beginnings you can provide will not only nourish your children in the moment but also for their entire lives.

As you delve into this world of nature with your child, remember young children don't yet have the same thinking capacities that you as an adult have. Young children live very deeply in imaginative pictures, not facts; intellectual thoughts will come at a later stage in their development. You don't need to explain the miracle of osmosis to your young child. You can say "Look, the sun fairies and the rain fairies came yesterday and fed the tiny shoots. Look how big they are today." Or say, "Look, how beautiful!" Or just silently pause and wonder at the magic of it all.

Don't forget, April can offer a sudden surprise! This year, after the snows of March melted, the last nor'easter of the season hit in the first week of April, dampening the spirits of those who were sure that those mid-March 50-60° days were the beginning of "real spring." Now, in mid-April, it seems "real spring" is here. Though the daffodils were bent flat under a foot of snow, they managed to pick themselves up and trumpet forth the glory of early mornings. Forsythia is now spraying yellow across the edges of lawns, and magnolias, flowering quince, and apple trees are beginning to show hints of color. Meanwhile, the air is filled with birdsong—the clear call of the cardinal, the cheery "Good Morning" of the robin, the perky "Hello" of the chickadee.

In the meadows, the lambs have raced out of the barns where they were born. The foals are chasing one another around the pastures. Bees are buzzing in the warm sunshine, and yes, the ants have started to appear in the kitchen. After the stillness of winter, across the land in New England the world of nature is in movement. Even the rocks and mud are sliding along in the rushing streams.

Your toddlers also want to be free to move. Whatever movements entice your children—as long as they are safe—set them free to explore. They will not only drink in the natural world with all their senses, the physical activities will contribute to building strong bodies and prepare them for academic learning. Your task is to encourage the natural movements—running, jumping, hopping, balancing, twirling, swinging. If your children are reticent about engaging in physical activities, turn outside time into a game you can also enjoy. Become hopping bunnies, racing squirrels, and galloping ponies with them. Later, plant some radishes, pansies in a pot or window box, or beans to later dry and shell. You are only limited by your imagination and your love of play.

After the constraints of freezing winds and innumerable layers of winter gear, the children are eager to get into motion, and much of their desire focuses on water. They are longing to stomp through puddles, to reshape the course of any flowing water, whether it be rushing stream or tiny rivulet. Oh, how joyful to drag a stick through a mud puddle and watch the swirls and spirals appear! Or later, take that same stick and drag away the leaves in the roadside swale to set the water free! Maybe it is simply running through the early morning dew, picking dandelions, or later in the day catching raindrops on their tongues as they merrily sail high on a swing. Perhaps it is even going outside in a warm spring rain wearing only their underwear.

Spring is indeed a watery season! Here in the Northeast, it falls in a wide variety of forms—perfect hexagonal snowflakes, mushy globs of white, ice pellets, sleet, freezing rain, drizzles, and downpours. All of these watery offerings fill up brooks, streams, ponds, and rivers while bringing forth life again to the hard, frozen earth of winter. Soon the mud begins to ooze round your boots, and puddles appear. This struggle between winter and spring is inevitable yet seems to take us by surprise each year. Our skin and hearts long for sunshine, warmth, and fresh air. Our souls are hungry for birdsong, flowers, and afternoons with friends. Most supermarket conversations at this time of year include some form of, "I'm tired of this. I'm sick of being cold. Enough already." It is easy to grow frustrated and impatient, to want to be finished with the tension of this struggle between the seasons.

Yet it is this very tension, this struggle that signals the earth to wake up. This tension between warmth and cold stimulates the sap in perennial plants and deciduous trees to slowly rise allowing the vegetation to wake up over time. And indeed, spring at last takes the upper hand. A green blush appears on the earth, bright yellow coltsfoot appears overnight and the birds begin to fill the air with song. Of course, next come the spring peepers sounding forth their cacophonous celebration of the season.

At the same time, this change of seasons asks for waiting, for patience. What does patience look like? Where do I see it in myself? Or rather, when am I not patient? One day last week I decided to brave the falling mixed precipitation and go outside. As I was walking by the pond near my house, I was drawn to observe its surface where either liquid snow or thick water was falling. At the point of impact of each falling white drop, concentric circles rippled outward, but it was happening slower than I remembered. I could actually watch the circles glide over and under each other, expanding until the whole surface of the water was covered with thousands of circles peacefully, patiently weaving over and under yet leaving the surface quite undisturbed.

Indeed, our patience is tested at this time of year in New England. At the same time that we are given the opportunity to expand our souls outward, we are called upon to find patience and equanimity to wait. It is not summer yet. We may still need our wool socks, hats and mittens. Even as we long for more sunshine, we have to patiently trust that it will arrive.

What about the children?

No patience there. They burst out. Out of their heavy clothes, out of the wintry elements, out of their houses.

We began with the melting snows of March, with water everywhere in all manner of forms in April. The children rush out. It is time for making mud pies, splashing in puddles, fishing in the streams, making rivers and dams in even the tiniest trickle of flowing water. The young child seeks to be one with the natural world, and what a wonderful time of year to let them experience all that is happening in the awakening world—smells, sounds, colors, textures, and even tastes. Let them get wet and muddy and later sample the first quiet violet they discover. They have little patience. I once observed my youngest child peel off his snowsuit, then sweater and overalls, and moments later one by one all the layers of wool only to roll naked in a mud puddle. Now that is becoming one with Nature!

Into the forest let us walk,
And see what wonders
Spring has brought.
Here's a flower
And there's a bee
And birds are singing
In every tree.

Oh, the glory of a New England spring!

MAY

Dancing into the Sun

It is hard to stay inside when the gentle rays of the May sun beckon us to come out and play. Never mind that those extra tasks on our to-do lists for cold winter days were never completed. The calls of the unsorted photographs, that unfinished sweater, the uncleaned closet in the back hall grow faint and can easily be ignored until next winter.

We and our children have been summoned outside to work in the yard, play catch, pick dandelions, and most of all move freely. As grown-ups we are called to walk, jog, and hike. The children are called to run, hop, jump, skip, spin, twirl, and tumble. How delightful to be able to move unencumbered by snowsuits, jackets, woolen hats, and all the rest! The little ones are mitten-free and can now use those fingers to pick tiny violet blossoms, sift sand from one hand to the other, and reach for the polka-dotted ladybug on a nearby leaf. The toddler can now sit on a swing and be pushed up and down, make mud pies and stir soups made of sand, leaves, sticks, and blossoms, and roll down grassy hills like a roly-poly rice ball.

For us as adults, it is not just our bodies that the sun summons. The warmth and sunshine of spring extend a welcoming invitation to our hearts and souls to enter deeply into the world of nature, to be nourished, filled by its beauty and wonder—the songs of the orioles and cardinals as they call forth the flowers and search for their mates, the delicate hues of apple blossoms, the bold faces of pansies, the fragrance of peonies. Our inner beings long for color, shape, and the experience of the transformation of the natural world. It is a time to breathe deeply and inhale the gifts that Mother Nature offers to us. Though it may seem a trite expression, it is important to "take time to smell the roses." Hidden among the petals are peace and serenity. What a feast a New England spring offers each of us!

It can be a challenge for us as caregivers of young children to "smell the roses" while also caring for our children. So many tasks, so many decisions to make that affect their futures. There are laundry, food shopping, baths, and bedtimes. There is time devoted to food preparation for a meal that may last only five minutes or may be rejected and never touched. There are falls, fevers, and squabbles. And what about making choices for their education, whether it is pre-school or college down the road?

In addition, our world seems to be in a topsy-turvy twirl at the moment; even the weather seems confused. For many years the saying was "April showers bring May flowers." This year it seems as though the April daffodils and tulips have brought the ongoing May showers. We can be grateful that through all of this, spring has prevailed and the world in New England is greening up. From day to day the grass grows greener and the trees leaf out. Just last week I could see my neighbor sitting in her yard enjoying the warmth of the morning sun. Yesterday she was hidden behind a screen of lilac blossoms and the fully leafed-out apple tree between us.

Even though I know it's coming, it surprises me every year: the amazement, the incredible, unbelievable miracle of unseen growing, the unimaginable amount of leaves which appear in just a few days. I find it impossible to comprehend the monumental amount of matter that is lifted up onto the tree branches in a few days. Each spring I am curious about how much actual leaf matter bursts forth from the hard dark skeleton of winter. This year my curiosity got the best of me; I went to Google. One maple tree three feet in diameter produces an estimated 100,000 leaves each year. One acre of mature, hardwood forest produces an estimated two tons of leaf matter, 4000 pounds of leaves. Isn't the world a miraculous place to be!

Your child may also be curious and ask, "Where do all the leaves come from?" "Aha," you say to yourself, "here is my chance to teach my child." You may be tempted to explain that freezing and thawing cause the sap to rise, a cell forms and then divides and divides, grows bigger as it prepares itself for photosynthesis.

This way of looking at the world can be abstract for young children, who live in the world of imagination. It may prematurely call upon forces of thinking while they are still living in a dreamy world of pictures and stories.

Let's slow down and take a different approach. Isn't it the warmth of the sun, the spring rains, and the nutrients in the soil that make the leaves? You may say yes, but how do you explain this unseen process to your child? Every day your child sees you doing work producing lunch, clean laundry or a mowed lawn. Who, then, are the workers who produce the leaves?

As adults, we can perhaps imagine that these unseen workers are forces, energies of warmth, and water, and physical matter which work together. One picture you can offer to your child is to give names to these forces and energies. For example, the energies that are at work in the soil can be called gnomes—beings who are busy tunneling in the soil, carrying the spring broth made by the water fairies to the roots. Then the sun fairies dance on the earth until the tree wakes up, the water fairies carry the broth to the top of the tree and the leaves begin to grow.

These energies have been named and honored in many countries for centuries. Most children today readily live into the reality of these beings. The children delight in imagining a little fellow with a big head, a red pointed cap, and a pick to move the rocks away from the roots or a flower fairy with a paint brush putting just the right color of yellow on the dandelions. Just as you feel at home with the facts, most children feel at home with the understanding that it is the "Little People" that make it happen. Children see these workers being busy helping to grow our food and make the world beautiful; they have a picture of how the forces in nature create our world. Later, in middle school and high school, they will learn a more scientific explanation for these phenomena, but underneath will be the richness of images that they drank in as young children.

Even if you lean towards the factual, the scientific, you may resonate with these ideas, but then wonder: How can I change the way I think and then respond to my child?

How to get on the same page as your child

After the winter, young children relish immersing themselves in nature, hungry to learn about the world, to experience the elements—earth, air, water, and the warmth of the sun. They come into the house wet, dirty, and happy. Some even want to become acquainted with the earth with every bit of themselves, so they proceed to roll naked in the mud, sand, or soft green grass. You need not be embarrassed; it is natural, and besides, fewer clothes means less laundry.

As children begin to explore the world outdoors and delight in the wonders of nature, they are also developing their body skills and capacities. Sometimes for parents, this can be scary. "Don't go too high." "Wait for me." "Take my hand." Yes, these warnings are sometimes necessary for the young child's safety. However, often these statements serve rather to address our fears as caregivers rather than the actual safety of the children. It is up to us as parents and caregivers to assess when precautions are necessary for the safety of the child and when it is about our ease. For the most part, as children turn towards four years of age, they know their bodies well enough to be able to assess their own concerns and limitations.

For example, when playing High Water, Low Water with a jump rope, children will be able to tell how high they want the rope held within an inch of their skill level. They will rarely climb up higher than they can get down. It is a matter of observing your child, and trusting when you can, and assisting when it is needed. Let them walk a balance beam unassisted; after all, a serious injury from six inches off the ground is unlikely. Let them explore the capacities of their limbs as well as the world. This is how they learn!

Things to do with your children

Suggestions for springtime activities for young children are not necessary. Just open the door and they will discover the world outside on their own. Following are some suggestions if you want to be engaged with them in their explorations.

• Take walks in parks and forests and suspend the scientific facts you know. Both when with your child and when alone, try to imagine the forces, the beings that have worked together to make spring happen.

• Find some children's books such as *The Tomten and the Fox*, *The Root Children*, and *The Gnome's Rosette* to share with your children.

• If you are gardening with your young child, planting radishes can be very satisfying. Unlike carrots and other food crops, radishes can be harvested in as little as three weeks from sowing.

• Gradually, as you think about this world of what can be called the world of elemental beings—of gnomes, fairies, and more—you can begin to make up your own stories as responses to your child's questions. For example, "Who makes the thunder?" "The rain fairies want to let us know that they are on their way to water the carrot seeds we planted yesterday. So, they took out their big drums and are drumming away." Once you get started down this path, your child may fill in the details for you.

• Find a little spot to build a gnome house; then let your imagination be free—acorn caps for porridge bowls, tiny sticks for spoons, dandelion fluff for mattresses.

- If at any moment your children ask a question and you are not certain how to respond or don't want to give a scientific explanation, you can always say, "I wonder!" Not only does this get you off the hook at the moment, it offers the children the opportunity to think for themselves what is happening. This statement encourages creative thinking on the children's part.

- If by chance you have one of those children who demand a scientific or factual answer and are satisfied with nothing less and "I wonder" doesn't satisfy, you can always explain, then add, "and the gnomes and water fairies are busy helping as well."

- During your walks you might even add, "Thank you, gnomes and fairies, for the green umbrella overhead which gives us shade."

Have fun! Enjoy your adventures!

JUNE

A Summer Symphony

"What is so rare as a day in June?" Though one may not be familiar with the poem by James Russell Lowell, a 19th century Boston poet, it is almost impossible not to experience rare June days here in New England, what I call Goldilocks Days, like the three bears' porridge—not too hot, not too cold, just right. These are the June days with an azure sky punctuated with cotton ball clouds, gentle breezes, blossoms, and birds. The air fills with the music of sights, sounds, and smells of the burgeoning earth. Along the wayside, nature offers up her delightful dance of daisies and lupines and the cheery song of cardinals. The earth is carpeted with color as iris, peonies, and fragrant roses parade forth in the garden. In the meadows breezes play over the grasses, creating eye-catching waves. Sunlight sparkles on stream and pond. The earth is generous as the symphony of early summer unfolds.

How wonderful for the young child to be bathed in this world of June! The joy of going out unencumbered in shorts, t-shirts, and bare feet. The delight in pouring sand from one hand to another, splashing in water, and filling every pocket with all manner of pebbles and stones. In fact, the child is not just walking over the earth but unconsciously being immersed in it, consuming it, in ways that are not possible for us in the same way as conscious adults. Young children literally become one with the earth—something that can be observed as the baby puts a pinch of sand into her mouth, or as the bath water drains from the tub at day's end, leaving a rim of dirt behind.

For children in June, time seems to slow down, even as nature is in a time of rapid growth. One can almost watch the leaves unfold and the flowers open. For children, too, summer is a time of growth. Their bodies grow bigger and stronger as they develop new skills. As the children are dressed in fewer layers, parents can almost see their limbs grow longer, and know that by September clothes will again no longer fit. As toddlers' bodies grow, nourished by digging and splashing, jumping and running, their inner life is also being fed by their outside adventures. The children are learning about life as nature reveals her secrets to them through their sense impressions. They are busy seeing, hearing, smelling, tasting, touching the world.

As parents and teachers, we also need to be nourished in our inner lives. By slowing down with the children, taking time to observe and listen, we, too, can hear the secrets the earth is whispering to us.

As James Russell Lowell continues:

And what is so rare as a day in June?
Then, if ever, come perfect days; ...
Whether we look, or whether we listen,
We hear life murmur, or see it glisten...

I hear the murmuring and see the glistening at the ocean. Every year I spend a week at summer's end at a beach on the coast of Maine. This year I had the opportunity to bookend the summer with five days on an island ten miles out to sea. Once there I instantly remembered why I love being at the ocean. With the first whiff of the tangy salt air, I feel I have come home. Like the fish and frogs that evolved over time as they moved onto the land, I always feel I evolve each time I step onto the sand and eventually into the water.

As I reflect, I realize what it is I so love about the ocean. For me the ocean is a healing, restoring, rejuvenating landscape. New Hampshire summers can be claustrophobic for me—rocks, weeds in my garden, and green leaves everywhere. When I get to the ocean, everything becomes simpler, more manageable. It doesn't matter if crumbs drop, or if I wear the same t-shirt three days in a row. The horizon is far away and the sky is a dome. There is space to move—move my body, move my soul.

I came to understand several years ago what is at the root of this expansiveness that comes to me with being at the ocean. The landscape itself is there in its simplicity; there is no overarching green canopy to distract me. The elements—earth, water, air, fire—are there in their essence—sand, sea, wind, sunshine. In addition, the four elements can be seen in relation to one another: the gentle haze as the wind blows the dry sand across the beach, the beautiful patterns on the sand left by the waves as they roll in, the sun sending slivers of gold across the surface of the water, the wind blowing the sea foam and ocean spray. I swim in essence, literally and figuratively.

I hiked to the cliffs overlooking the Atlantic, where waves crashed on the rocks far below. As I gazed east over the vast ocean, I saw something challenging to find here in hilly New Hampshire: the stark clarity of the unbroken horizon line, a straight boundary dividing sea and sky, heaven and earth. There was nothing made by humans in my outward view, only what had been given by the Creator. Then came the comfort of the song of the ceaseless tide! I could leave my worries and the world with its disturbing events behind and rest for a few moments in peace and gratitude. I felt a softening, an expanding of my soul.

As you plan your summer, I encourage you to make time to be at the ocean. Whether for day visits or an extended stay, you can find healing and nourishment for you and your children. You can feel rested and restored. Hopefully you will have another adult with you to watch the children, so you can have some solitary time to walk or sit on a rock and watch the tides. The ocean provides a place for contemplation. You may find inspiration, new thoughts about your life, perhaps an awareness of a way in which you would like to change your caregiving style, or becoming aware of new projects you would like to undertake. This summer, make some space for the ocean to move your soul.

As for the children they will be joyful, happy as they become one with the elements. When they have a bucket, shovel, and the bounty of the ocean's gifts, your challenges will also be simple—how to get them out of the water, how to get them to come to the blanket for lunch, and how to get them to stand still so you can apply sunscreen.

Yes, July is a time to slow down and drink in all that nature has to offer us. For me, for many years now, it has been the ocean where I return to rest and find soul nourishment. For you it may be a different landscape; perhaps a lake, a forest, the mountains. Whenever it is possible, take your children and go home this summer—to the ocean, the mountains, the forest. In the future it may not be their place for rest and peace, but they will feel your joy of return, your memories, and they will love to hear your stories. They will experience through you what going home feels like. Share with them the joy which fills your soul. At the same time, you will be giving them a treasure, a peek into who you are.

Join your children

So why not join your young children on these rare June days? Go outside and soak up what nature has to offer. Your children do this naturally. If this is not already a habit you have, you may need to decide to do it consciously. But don't miss what June has to offer to you. Go slowly! Take time to hear what murmurs and see what glistens!

• Sit on the beach and pour warm sand from one hand to another.

• As you walk in the water at a lake or the ocean, skim each foot across the surface and watch the round drops rise and cascade down like a river of pearls.

• Stop by the roadside and see the wave patterns on the grasses as the breezes change direction.

• Watch for the first firefly of the season.

• Stand outside under the full moon before heading off to bed.

• Find a berry patch and experience the sweet taste of summer.

• Delight in the dance of the dragonflies as they dip and fly.

• Make a daisy chain crown for your toddler.

- Sit beside a campfire and watch the flames twist and twirl.

- Gather fallen flower petals, crush them in water with a stone, then dye a piece of cheesecloth, gauze, or a piece of an old cotton t-shirt. Hang it to dry then stitch it into a tiny pouch.

- Take up gardening, even if it is only one tomato plant in a pot. Getting one's hands into the earth is very grounding and can help reduce anxiety and elevate one's mood. Eating a tomato you have grown yourself feeds your soul as well as your body.

- Offer gratitude to the earth for her wonders.

Remember, opportunities for your child to get to know the world expand exponentially in the summer. Have fun and enjoy the symphony of summer!

Summer School for Toddlers

Throughout life, the human being is engaged in getting to know the world. For teenagers this focuses on expanding their thinking in new ways. For the school age child, even while learning is occurring, the world of feelings is deeply experienced and explored—happiness, sadness, love, hate, hurt, disappointment, excitement, rhythm, and beauty. From the moment of birth, the work of the young child is to learn about the physical world, the world of earth, water, air, and fire.

Summer in New England is a most wonderful time and place to explore these substances that make up our physical world. Outside in the open air, toddlers can give free rein to experiencing and experimenting with earth, water, and air. Indeed, the natural world is the Summer School Classroom for young children.

Earth—a sand box, a mud pit, a pile of rocks, a garden bed. What can be learned there? A rock is heavier than a handful of sand, lifting a rock takes more energy than lifting a pebble. An arm bends at the wrist to add sand to the sand castle but it does not bend between the wrist and the elbow. Sticks break but limbs don't. Fine sand goes through a sifter but pebbles do not. Sand in the sun gets too hot to walk on in bare feet. Toes scatter dry sand. Toes sink into squishy sand. Toes stand firm on sand pounded by the surf.

Water—a brook, a stream, a watering can, a sprinkler, a hose, a lake, the ocean. What can be learned there? Water runs away. It can be hot or cold; it can gush from the earth or fall from the sky; it can make a trench or mud puddle. It can wash away a sand castle. It can't be easily held in one's hand. In a sand pail with petals and berries it can turn purple or yellow. As a dewdrop in the morning sun it offers rainbows to the world.

Air—the rascally element, invisible: a breeze, a wind, a storm. A kite, a bird, a pinwheel, a balloon, a butterfly, a cloud. What can be learned about the unseen element? Air brings objects into movement. It can be hot or cold. It can sing, shout, or whisper. Air makes the June grasses wave Good Morning; it makes the pansies nod Hello. It picks up dry sand but not rocks. When called forth by a paper fan it cools the face.

Fire—a lighted match, a candle flame, a lantern, a camping stove, a campfire, fireworks, lightning. Fire is hot. It flashes and sparks, it dances and spirals and spins and then it disappears. It can release flames or smoke; when contained, it is delightful to watch. When it gets big it gets scary. It can help or harm. "When there is fire, I need a grown-up."

This learning is derived from sensations, observations, and being immersed in experiences. The young child soaks up the world like a sponge absorbing water. Conscious thought is a dim shadow on the horizon. Taking in the world is a process that proceeds on its own; sensory impressions collect in the child's body, awaiting the addition of facts and concepts as intellectual capacities come to the forefront in adolescence.

It is then that the child begins to add understanding to what has until then lived in the physical body and in memories.

The see-saw that I played on as a child was a lever; the slide was an inclined plane. Having Sally on my lap when going down the slide helped me go faster because of the co-efficient of friction and gravity.

Waves don't pile up on the beach, because liquids seek a level surface. Salad dressing needs to be shaken, because left on their own oil and vinegar don't mix and the heavy liquid sinks to the bottom. The rock I put under the boulder I wanted to excavate held it up so I could get the board under it, and now I can wedge a board under the piano legs so that I can slide the new rug underneath it.

Dandelions are fun to play with, but blowing on them is a means for seed dispersal; now my yard is filled with golden flowers in May.

In the years dedicated to intellectual learning, adolescents learn details, specifics, names. They learn that the human body is made up of approximately 60% water; the brain and kidneys 85%, the heart and lungs 75%, the bones 25%, and the teeth 8%. They learn that the jump ropes, buckets, and limbs that they used to lift rocks made a simple pulley and that the curlicue that helped the beach umbrella stay upright is called a screw. They see that the salt in the soup did not go away but only changed its form; when heated with a Bunsen burner until the broth was gone, it could reappear. Oh, and by the way, the dandelion is a dicotyledon.

Infants can feed themselves for many months before they can say "spoon" or "cracker." They pull off footwear many months before they can say "sock" or "shoe." First, the experience, then the words, only later the concepts. This same process occurs as young children learn about the world in which they live. First the experience, then the words, then the concepts. The experiences that children have in nature are rooted in their bodies and are the foundation on which facts can find a home later in the elementary and high school years.

Open the door and go outside with your young children this summer! Give them the opportunity to learn physics, biology, chemistry, math, the four elements, the life cycles. Enroll your child in Science 101!

Song of the Dandelion

Dandelion all yellow and gold,
what do you do all day?
I sit and I wait in the tall green grass
'til the children come to play.

Dandelion all yellow and gold,
what do you do all night?
I sit and I wait in the tall green grass
'til my hair turns long and white.

And what do you do when your hair turns white
and the children come to play?
They take me up in their dimpled hands
and they blow my hair away.

—Anonymous

SUMMER —

AIR

Every child is a different kind of flower,
and all together,
make this world a beautiful garden.

    —Rumi

JULY

Wonder and Gratitude

Summer is certainly a season of wonder! Everywhere we look, we see new leaves, new blossoms, new fruits. From day to day the landscape and garden change. The varied greens of the spring trees give way to a forest of dark green. Flowers burst forth in garden and roadside in a grand display of color. And it is not just eyes that are awakened. Ears also are on alert—frogs croak on the evening pond, hummingbird wings whir as they zoom in for a sunset cocktail, and a platoon of bees buzzes through the lavender and milkweed. Indeed, the earth is a feast for all the senses. Soft grass tickles the toes as tiny fingers pluck leaves that are smooth or soft and fuzzy. Pungent mint and delicate roses offer their perfumes. What about the taste of July's first tomatoes, and sweet corn dripping with butter?

Unless one is totally consumed by some unexpected sorrow or overwhelmed by the practicalities and responsibilities of parenting young children, it is almost impossible to be oblivious to the wealth of sense impressions offered by the earth in midsummer. She gives freely, with no expectation of receiving anything in return, while nourishing our bodies and souls. As eyes and ears are drawn out into the world of nature, we are stirred by the beauty and wonder of it all—from the barely visible tiny red spider to a glorious orange sunset, and perhaps, if we are lucky, a late afternoon thunderstorm followed by a rainbow. Our hearts, too, are drawn out, our souls reaching for the sun. There is no limit to the wonders of the world of nature in summer.

The young child is at one with this world, drinking in its beauty and wonder, like a thirsty sponge, as food for body and soul. The baby sits on the beach contentedly pouring sand from one hand to another, and the toddler gathers pockets of pebbles, as the three-year-old jumps, hops, runs, twirls, and rolls over the ground. Wonder and delight abound!

As adults, our responsibilities can often have us moving through this wonderful world without taking in the wonder and beauty of it all. However, making moments to slow down and move at the same speed as the little ones gives not only the opportunity to appreciate nature's gifts but also a moment to give back for the wonder and beauty we have received. We can offer gratitude for what has been so generously given.

For us as adults, fostering this attitude of gratitude can be a support beyond the garden walls. As we go through our days, the sense of gratitude for what we receive and what comes to us can offer moments of calm as we go forward with our daily tasks and challenges. In giving thanks we can connect with something greater than ourselves, with hope and grace. A sense of peace and well-being can begin to permeate our inner lives.

Occasionally one can make this mood of gratitude more concrete for ourselves and for our children by actually saying the words of gratitude aloud. While walking through the garden or along the shore, say "Thank you, birds, for your beautiful songs." "Thank you, little brown toad for hopping in my yard. I am happy you like living in my garden." "Wow! What a golden butterfly!" Or join arms with your children around a tree and say, "Thank you, tree, for giving us shade." These words of wonder will connect you with your children, for they, too, are experiencing the wonder and delight of the natural world. At the same time, your words will model for them a feeling of gratitude for all that is received. Supporting your children in developing this mood of gratitude is a gift to them for their whole lives.

In her poem "Sometimes," after describing a midsummer lightning storm, Mary Oliver offers us a doorway into gratitude:

> *Instructions for living a life:*
> *Pay attention.*
> *Be astonished.*
> *Tell about it.*

I had such a wonder-filled moment this July. It was high summer, the roadsides aflame with orange lilies. The heat of the day was sticky on my skin. Baby turkeys were following in a row behind their mother across the road into the meadow.

There were no adult turkeys behind; they had all gone ahead. Yet the baby turkeys wobbled forward in a straight line. Mother turkey trusted that her babies would follow her, learning how to be a turkey as they go. It is in their DNA to be a turkey.

So, it is with our children. Their specific DNA is determined at the moment of conception. Much of their physicality is already fixed before they are born. Soon after birth, the comments begin: "Does she look like her dad?" "He has his mother's eyes and dimples." "She is going to be tall like her mom." Heredity is one factor in forming a human being.

At the moment of birth, a second element comes to the fore. The children, like the young turkeys, begin to follow along behind us as they learn to be human beings. In the beginning, their lives depend on our care. With their first breath, it becomes our responsibility to provide them with the experiences most supportive of their becoming a well-rounded, healthy human being. This period of becoming extends over 16 to 21 years or even longer. Unlike the baby turkeys, who in a few days are able to move about seeking food, human babies require years to develop the necessary skills to survive.

Once on earth, like sponges, human babies and small children drink in what their adults choose for them. Every sense impression imprints itself upon these young beings; whatever they experience becomes a part of them. As yet they have no capacity to screen out what is not supportive of their growing. The color and feel of their clothing, the quality of the food they eat, and even the feelings in your heart as you move through the day affect them, shaping them. The inner and outer sense impressions from their environment are a second factor that contributes to who each child becomes.

Like the baby turkeys, human beings are formed and shaped by their heredity and their environment. However, human beings have a third aspect that contributes to who they become, an invisible element. It is the unique individuality, the essence that each human being carries within his or her heart. It is the thing that makes you YOU. The thing that enables the two-year-old having a tantrum to say "I do it." Nobody else can claim it. Nobody else has one like it. It is that part of each of us that goes with us through life whatever our DNA and early childhood experiences have given us. The journey of each individual is unlike that of every other human being. In freedom we can make choices, not only out of the givens of heredity and environment, but also out of our own individual essence. Although this essence is only observable to a small degree in the early years, as the child continues to grow and mature more and more of this individual essence becomes visible.

What does this mean for parents? The heredity has been determined; the sense impressions of the environment are being chosen for the most part by you. What is your responsibility as a parent for that third element, the unique individuality of your child? What do you do as parents to support the healthy development of your child's essence?

Watch, listen, and wait. It is your child's unique journey and will only be revealed over time. While you wait, slow down and observe what your child is showing you, either in actions or in words. Children will gradually begin to inform you about who they are. Eventually, you may even be graced with a glimpse of who they will become as adults.

In addition to observing and listening, you can provide an environment that fosters exploration and discovery. In the early years, you can provide them with opportunities to explore the natural world, materials for art making, and abundant time to play freely. It is in this early childhood period, when imaginative play is blossoming, that the young child begins to explore the activities that human beings do.

They will try on many hats, play many roles. As they get older, they will see more and more activities in which human beings can engage.

The young child explores who she is through play. Play is a crucial element in a young child's early years. In play they practice social skills including sharing, caring for others, and building relationships. Their capacity for imagination explodes, and they learn to solve problems—both emotional issues and questions of physical construction as they build houses and forts with others. All of this in a relaxed, easy-going manner. They apply themselves with energy and vigor, much as healthy adults do when they take up the tasks of their chosen work. In fact, play is the work of the young child.

You may want your child to take up your profession, make the same choices that you have made, share your values; however, the unfolding of each human is individual, unlike any other. Your child at the age of ten may know her journey calls her to become an airplane pilot. It may not be until your son takes a particular university course that he gets a clue about what he will love to do that will give meaning to his life. Perhaps your eighteen-year-old child will meet someone who offers a thought essential to their journey of self-exploration. Maybe at age twenty, a relationship will develop that will continue for your child's entire life.

However the journey unfolds, it is your child's story. How exciting to be a part of that journey!

Make time to offer gratitude for the wonder and delights of July. Make time to offer gratitude for the wonder that is your child.

AUGUST

Savoring the Last Bites

After a gentle spring, summer has blasted in with hot, humid days and nights that don't cool down. Too hot to sleep! Too hot to cook! Too hot to eat! Too hot to think! Staying hydrated has taken on a new urgency.

With the summer sun and frequent rains this year, the plants are growing and fruiting, offering a feast for the senses—colors, shapes, tastes, and smells. Birds offer sweet melodies, bees buzz, dragonflies swoop and sail, and the crickets and katydids sing into the night. Here, in New England, the earth is fully awake and alive in the summer.

In outer nature, this intense heat seems to be hurrying natural processes. Flowers that usually bloom in September are already drying up. Goldenrod, which typically blooms in early August, can be spotted as early as mid-July. The first red maple leaves, which begin to show in late August, could already be seen in late July.

In fact, the entire world is heating up. Whatever one's

position on climate change, the air around us is getting observably hotter. The political scene throughout the world is getting hotter, too. National and international events are happening at a pace that is challenging to understand or process. Every day seems to bring a new crisis or catastrophe.

Yet human beings long for calm and peace. Summer's gift is a most welcome invitation to slow down, to make spaces for peace and calm. The heat tells us to slow down. There is a longing to savor the sunshine and ease of summer—beauty all around, relaxed times with friends and family, and the ease of fewer clothes and gear to manage or snow to shovel. Summer offers innumerable opportunities to relish what surrounds us outside and moments to connect with those we love.

At the same time, as human beings, we may grow a bit sleepy. As the days grow hotter and the humidity higher, we tend to slow down and take life a bit easier. Our list of tasks for the day may be usurped by a trip to a lake for swimming or a picnic lunch under the shade of an apple tree. The children may sleep in a little; you may sit a while sipping your morning coffee as you watch the hummingbirds sip from the feeder. Although there are still meals to prepare and laundry to fold, in due time, everything gets completed in the "lazy, hazy days of summer."

Within this slowed-down pace of living, there can be moments to savor and relish. If we take the time to gather a blanket, a few picture books, and snacks, a delightful afternoon can be spent in the backyard shade. A trip to the beach with ice cream for dinner may be just the thing for a steamy day. This slowed-down pace of the adults gives the children permission to slow down, to refresh, to recharge, and even to grow. Growth spurts often occur in the summer. Parents may not see the changes, as they are with the children every day.

However, they are shocked at the differences when they bring out the long pants and sweaters as the coolness of autumn begins to settle in.

Slowing down also allows us to take in the details of what Mother Nature offers. We can gaze with astonishment at her shapes and forms—the intricate Fibonacci spiral in sunflowers, the exquisite curves in garlic scapes, the hidden star beneath each scabiosa petal. We see the glorious pinks, lavenders, and bright yellows of zinnias, the brilliant red of tomatoes, the bold orange pumpkins. Our eyes feast on summer's offerings as our souls are nourished.

Yet there is the possibility of slowing down even more. Instead of allowing the sense impressions to stop at our eyes, we can let them sink deeper. We can allow them to move into our hearts as we submit in wonder at the transcendent order and beauty around us. Each new flower can be a gift, a miracle, moving our hearts with wonder. As this wonder wells up, it can move our hearts to overflow with gratitude for the life and world we have been given.

Adults may sometimes forget about wonder, but young children go through their days in wide-eyed wonder. Since their task is to get to know the world, they drink in everything around them; they let it fill every pore. They are happy to run through the garden or down the forest path. Yet, if something catches their attention, they stop and give their whole selves over to what they see, whether it's a dandelion, a butterfly, or a tiny pebble. Then again, it is not just one pebble; it is every pebble. Each one is a wonder to be treasured and tucked into a pocket.

This quality of being present in young children is a gift to parents and caregivers. They remind us to slow down and be present with the wonder of the world ourselves. Not only do we get to experience their delight at each wonder, but we have the opportunity to experience the wonder of whatever it is they are seeing—bug, daisy, or milkweed fluff.

In August, as growth, fruiting, and harvesting intensify, there is much for adults and children to drink in. Slowing down to take in this wonder offers us intimate moments with our children. In addition, for busy parents, it can offer peace, beauty, and joyful memories for the cold winter days. Filling our hearts with wonder can nourish souls, relieve stress, and even lower blood pressure. Wonder is itself a wonder drug.

May you be filled with the wonders of the last weeks of summer!

I had such moments to savor this summer. I spent an entire day with my adult daughter beside a crystal clear, cold, snow-fed mountain river. We watched a mother duck swim upstream and then back down with her six ducklings. Five of them followed right behind as she took them to a sheltered place in the reeds to feed. Number six went off exploring on her own into some bushes. Suddenly, she realized she had been left behind and rapidly paddle-wheeled her little feet to catch up. We chuckled at the same time at this comic image.

We watched the pure white clouds sail over and the moving sun change the shadow patterns on the trees. We soaked our feet in the icy river, imagining that just a few weeks earlier, the water had been fifteen feet of snow on the peaks of the high Sierras. We observed the swirls and splashes as the river raced over the rocks, and we climbed over the granite boulders at the water's edge. We wondered how the large, round potholes had been created in the granite slab.

We savored those precious moments in nature as well as the precious moments as mother and adult daughter. A feast of a day!

As I reflect on that day, one of my favorite children's stories comes to mind, *Frederick* by Leo Lionni. Frederick is a mouse who lives with his family. As summer draws to a close, all of the mice except Frederick scurry around gathering food for the winter ahead. Not Frederick. He sits and stares. When questioned, he replies, "I am gathering colors." Frederick was quite wise for a little mouse! After all, aren't colors as important for us in deep December as soup and sandwiches?

As you slow down, in the coming hot, humid days, look for moments of color that you can carry into next winter. Perhaps it will be watching a bee sip nectar, a butterfly hatch from its chrysalis, a field of grass blown by the wind, a bouquet of flowers you have grown yourself, a trip to see relatives, a picnic at a nearby lake at sunset, staying up late to watch for shooting stars, observing a hill of ants moving their eggs after being disturbed. Whatever it is, slow down and be prepared to be amazed at the world.

You might recall one such moment in February when you find yourself longing for summer's warmth. Maybe one of these moments will even appear in a bedtime story on some cold, frosty night.

In the meantime:

- Make one more trip to the beach.

- Go blackberry picking.

- At a farm stand, get a local, juice-running-down-to-the-elbows peach.

- Swim at a nearby lake.

- Try on the fall clothes and celebrate with your children how much they have grown.

- Take an after-dinner stroll and listen to the crickets.

- Go to a farmers' market and enjoy the colors and abundance.

- Mark the end of summer with one last trip for ice cream.

- Eat corn-on-the-cob and watermelon.

- Gather a bouquet of summer flowers.

A young child once said to me, "The bees are sipping the sweet summer." With your children, sip the last sweet days of summer and savor them.

SEPTEMBER

Gathering Abundance

Autumn has approached once again in the round of the seasons. The delicate lavenders and pinks of summer have given way to the vibrant colors of fall. The season of growth is passing as the natural process of decay and dying accelerates, while the earth offers up her fruits. Now it is harvest time.

I look in amazement at the glory of what nature has condensed and pours forth for my nourishment and delight. What a wonder! Pumpkins have come to their fullness, glowing bright vermillion and orange out from the dying leaves. Zinnias give up their final hurrah with a burst of sunbeam colors. Trees are laden with crisp, juicy red apples, promising pies. Bright red peppers, deep purple beets, orange carrots, forest green curly kale, and winter squash in a variety of colors and shapes abound. The deep blue sky accentuates the golds of corn shocks, fading grasses, and sweet pears. Sparks of color paint the horizon as milkweed feathers float in the air. Acorns sound a drumbeat for summer's departure.

During the summer, as I watched my garden change from day to day, I found a renewed interest in the forms found in nature. Each tiny cherry tomato offered a star at the point where it grew from its stem; the sunflowers, a spiral. Now I stand in awe as I pick the dried seed heads from my scabiosa flowers. Each head is formed of small cups packed together into a globe, which reminds me of drawings by M. C. Escher—no spaces between, everything connected. Then comes the surprise of discovering the globe is a galaxy, for tucked into each small cup is a perfect five-pointed star.

My interest in the forms found in nature continued when I spent the first week of September rediscovering forms at the ocean. Each day, the tides shared stories and treasures in the shapes of seashells, fluffy gull feathers, and sunbeams dancing in the surf. I saw the story of the ocean's night journey in the patterns left in the sand, swirls, squiggles, potholes, and ridges. There was the morning delight of discovering the new Celtic designs created by the periwinkles as they snail across the sand. So much for each human being to discover and rediscover.

Now, as autumn delivers her vast store of wares, there is more to discover and savor. A new fragrance is in the air. There is a sense of excitement and impending change. Even though nature around is fading, decaying, dying, there abounds color and beauty—crisp morning air, clear golden light, bright blue skies. Who among us can fail to feel joy and a sense of well-being at this time of year? At the same time, for adults, there can be another stirring in the soul, an unrest, an uneasiness, an awareness of changes to come.

During the warm days of summer, the souls of human beings have been drawn outward. Their hearts have been nourished by the season of growing, ripening, and the joyful gatherings of family and friends, by birds and bees and blossoms. Summer has been a time of expanding and giving in to warmth and fun, of dreaming through the hazy summer days.

But what of the soul of the human being at this time of the equinox? Is the fading of nature a portent of the fading of human awareness also? Will we, like the plants in our gardens, fall asleep? It is the challenge at this time of year, when the sunlight recedes and sharper shadows appear, to not fall asleep but, as human beings, to wake up. If we awaken, however, we may find that sharper shadows, dragons, lurk in our unconscious. In our thoughts and deeds, these shadowy dragons of unconsciousness may rear their heads as judgment, criticism, blame, lack of commitment, unkind words, fear, greed, thoughtlessness, or apathy. There is no standard dragon. Its form is unique to each individual. Your dragon, what is yours to transform, is not the same as mine. While I may struggle with judging others, you may struggle with a lack of commitment.

In these moments of recognizing and acknowledging our dragons, it is essential to remind ourselves that the dragon is not to be feared, but is our friend; the dragon gives us information about the true human being beneath the spines and prickles of our shadow side. By facing the shadow, by bringing awareness of the forces hindering our growth into the light of our consciousness, there is the possibility of seeing in which direction to turn to find our true selves. By shining the light of consciousness on the dragons in our souls, we can be the vehicle for meeting and understanding the forces that rob us of our power. Through our striving to live from a place of compassion for ourselves and others, we open our hearts to becoming the persons we are meant to be.

In centuries past in many cultures, this turning point was marked by the festival of Michaelmas. The figure of the Archangel Michael as depicted in works of art shows him thrusting his sword to hold down and tame a shadowy dragon, taking away its ability to do harm. In these images we can see parallels to the legend today if we look into the shadows both outside and inside ourselves and seek the dragons. We are reminded to wake from summer's dream, to pay attention, to look around, to look into the shadows, to welcome our dragons for what they can tell us about ourselves. If we strive to transform our dragons by facing them head-on, something within each one can stir, and that which is truly human—the soul-spiritual element—can awaken. With a reawakened awareness and new energy, humans can turn inward and allow the deepest parts of their beings to come to the forefront once again.

Autumn can be a moment to take up this call and, with clarity in thought and courage in heart, seek to understand the truth, mystery, beauty, and wonder of life.

Don't worry! I have not forgotten the children. That comes next.

For the child from birth to three, the whole world is at their fingertips, and it is theirs to discover. This discovery of the world begins with the first in-breath, and is the foremost task of the child from birth to age three. They have been invited into a mysterious world in which everything is new: new tastes, new smells, new sounds. In addition to discovering the world around them, they have the task of discovering who they are and learning what their bodies can do: finding their hands as a first toy, rolling, sitting, standing, walking, and talking. What enormous tasks they have before them. For the young child, life is all about exploration and discovery. I want to know about the world I have landed in.

Later, as adolescents, they will begin to take up other realms of discovery. Who am I? Where is my journey taking me?

How can we, as parents and caregivers, support these young beings in their quest to discover the world and themselves? In autumn, so much is happening outside that excites and delights the young child. Being outdoors together offers time to connect and share the delicious wonders of this season with them.

Let them explore as much as they can on their own, as you stand by to offer safety and assistance as needed. They will surprise you with what they can do. And indeed, there is much to discover—heavy/light, hard/soft, smooth/rough, warm/cold, up/down, forwards/backwards, can do it/not yet.

Invite them into, welcome them to, introduce them to the physical world. Say "Look," "Wow," and "How amazing."

Offer them opportunities to explore moving the world and their bodies in new ways. Take them to hills to roll down. Take them on walks in orchards and forests this autumn so they can gather acorns and go crunch, crunch through the dried leaves.

Apple picking can be a delightful activity as the children toddle beneath the trees laden with shiny red orbs, wandering as they go, picking up one, then another, then another, filling a basket to take home.

Take one of those apples and slice it between the stem and the bottom. Let them discover the star inside. Do it again and again. The wonder of a star inside each apple! At the same time, you can rediscover wonder at the star inside.

Choose from a field or farm stand just the right pumpkin or two to bring color into the home.

Whenever possible, dig up a few potatoes or carrots, and find something to harvest.

Pick the last flowers in the garden and along the roadside, grind them with a rock, add water to make soup for the dollies, or make dye to add color to bits of cheesecloth.

Walk in a forest gathering leaves, lichen, and bits of bark—the stuff of future projects or objects for the nature table.

Catch a falling leaf and make a wish on it.

Exploring the world of nature with young children is a wonderful way to introduce them to the physical world and to what their bodies can do. These explorations offer moments for wonder and gratitude, so their souls are also nourished and can grow. You may find moments to pause in silence or with a quiet comment to acknowledge the awe and wonder of your discoveries. You, as well as your children, will be nourished.

So much for each human being to discover and rediscover!

Rhythm, Ritual, and the Unexpected

Do you remember longing for a "good old-fashioned winter"? Do you remember when it got cold you put on the woolies and didn't take them off until April? Do you remember when a "Snow Day" was called because ten inches of snow had fallen during the night? Unfortunately, if you like winter, now it is more likely a two-hour delay because the air has warmed and a slight drizzle has glazed the roads.

Back then, there was the *rhythm* of getting ready for bed in the winter: putting on clean underwear before all the layers—long johns, turtlenecks, and PJs—to be ready for school the next morning, then just exchanging the PJs for long pants or overalls and a wool sweater. Having all the under layers on was a bonus at 6:30 am when it was ten degrees Fahrenheit outside and the wood stove hadn't quite caught up.

Caregivers of young children quickly learn that rhythm helps carry the children and themselves through the day. Everybody knows what is coming next, so everybody gets in the flow: get dressed, eat breakfast, play outside, eat snack, play inside, eat lunch, take a nap ... and so it goes through the day. Rhythm helps the caregiver guide the children through the day and week. It is helpful in that it avoids the necessity of explaining what comes next. The repetition offers the children predictability and safety. They experience, "We did it this way yesterday, and the day before, and the day before that. Now we will do it the same way today." The children are able to relax and not be concerned because they know what comes next.

Rhythms, whether daily, weekly, or monthly, are often connected to the calendar. Whatever their frequency, the regular recurrence offers a developing sense of trust in life. "The world is good."

There are other events that may happen within the scope of regular daily or weekly rhythms; we can call these *rituals*. They themselves are not part of a calendar rhythm but happen within it—for example, lighting a candle and offering gratitude before a meal.

There are other events which happen not related to the flow of the yearly calendar. These rituals have a rhythm of their own. They are often connected with birthdays, holidays, or religious celebrations, or they may even be tied to random events. For example, I remember those earlier days before weather patterns shifted and winters were intense. When I announced "No school!" my three children jumped out of bed, delighted to be able to stay in their pajamas. They raced down the stairs to see if the expected blueberry pancakes with warm maple syrup were ready. I say "expected" because a snow day automatically meant pancakes for breakfast. It was a family tradition. My children still remember those slow-moving mornings. They also remember climbing the stairs each evening in the dark during Advent, the four weeks before Christmas, each child headed to bed carrying a lighted candle while singing a carol.

The pancake ritual and the Advent ritual happened within our family, as *family rituals*. There are other rituals that take place within the context of larger groups, festival celebrations, religious services, meetings or gatherings directed to a particular grouping of people: *community rituals*.

My children also remember the storm that brought enough snow to build a castle with walls four feet high in our front yard. They remember after dinner we all put on snow gear and went out to the castle. There we lit candles tucked into little snow niches and ate warm bread pudding made by Grandma in the afternoon. This was a happening that came together totally spontaneously. A big snowfall, a grandma who loved to bake, parents who were rested and were willing to take on getting everyone into winter gear again, a stash of tea lights, and a dark sky filled with stars made for a happening that came together spontaneously. *The unexpected.*

In the midst of rhythm and ritual, who doesn't enjoy a surprise, something new punctuating the rhythm, an unexpected and happy event. The unexpected can offer joy and delight, a spark of light before a return to the rhythm. These occurrences are often the substance of children's memories.

Ah! Memories. Parents want to offer their children a life rich with experiences to remember as well as to enjoy in the moment. We want to offer them moments or daily rituals vivid enough that they will recollect them with warmth and delight. Perhaps when they have children of their own they will do things the same way.

Memories! How do they embed themselves in our children's minds? We cannot choose what our children remember. Their memories are connected to their individual beings. Something in each child selects what to recollect when they are older. It is an individual process that we cannot control. It has been documented many times that even siblings have different—sometimes even opposite—recollections of the same event. We provide the experiences and each child selects the memories.

Rhythm and *ritual* carry us along through our days, and *the unexpected* wakes us up to something new and exciting.

What can we do for the children?

Rhythm

Daily living itself provides opportunities for offering rhythm, for example:

- Wake up, eat breakfast, get dressed, play, snack, play, lunch, nap, etc.

- Every Saturday, visit grandparents.

- Monday is mac and cheese night, Wednesday is vegetable soup, Friday is pizza, and Sunday breakfast is French toast or bagels and cream cheese.

- Thursday is Story Hour at the library.

Do whatever works for you and the children to offer ease, predictability and stability.

Ritual

Rituals are often connected with birthdays, holidays, or festival celebrations.

- Offer special poems or songs, offerings of gratitude, traditional foods.

- Honor the seasonal festivals with candles.

- Build a fire outside at the solstices—winter and summer.

- Invite the children to choose what they want for dinner on their birthdays.

- Light a candle and say a blessing before the evening meal.

- Make Valentine's cards with your children to give to neighbors.

Do whatever is in alignment with your values and beliefs that you want to pass along to your children.

The Unexpected

Limited only by your imagination!

- Bring out a toy that you have put away for a while because your child was too young for it earlier.

- Take a special trip or vacation or go on an outing on the spur of the moment.

- Have a Pajama Day!

- Put the child in a bathtub or wading pool when tempers flare. This can take a child by surprise and help to shift the mood for both of you.

- Step out into nature, which offers many opportunities for the unexpected.

- Allow your young child to stand outside naked in a warm spring rain—of course, only if circumstances permit.

- When your child is ready for bed and it is a cold, dark winter night and the stars are dancing in the sky, dress your child in a warm hat and jacket and stand on the porch for a couple of minutes.

- Build a giant snow person, turtle, dragon, rabbit, boat, cat or castle.

- Cover your lawn with snow angels that both you and your children make.

- In summer at the beach build a giant castle, turtle, or bunny.

What can we do to care for ourselves?

Grownups also need rhythm, ritual, and the unexpected in their lives.

Establish a daily, weekly *rhythm* for your family. It will help to carry you and your children along through the day and to alleviate stress that comes with parenting young children.

Make a daily rhythm that includes at least five minutes for you to gather your forces, perhaps in the morning before the day begins.

Include five minutes at the end of the day, when you are not falling asleep, to reflect on the day. What went well? What could be different tomorrow?

Plan ahead for special occasions by establishing rituals and traditions. Your life will be less hectic and stressful.

Treat yourself to the unexpected. Of course, with young children in your care, it cannot be totally spontaneous, but perhaps you can on the spur of the moment arrange an outing. Consider a spa day, a night out with friends, purchasing that book or art supply you have been wanting, calling a neighbor to watch your children while you go for a walk, getting a babysitter at the last moment and taking your partner or a friend out to a movie or for an evening walk.

Anything that offers you care, nourishment, and relaxation!

Like the stones, we have bodies made of minerals. Like the plants, we have life. Like the plants, we breathe in and out, and have life-giving fluids in our veins. These living processes take place in a rhythm. Like the animals, we have feelings. Animals have feeding and mating rituals, as humans often plan rituals to connect with family happenings or religious services. Only human beings have the ability to say "I," have the capacity to choose, to move themselves out of a flow and do something different, the unexpected. Being mindful of both our need for a strong rhythmical structure to our life and our capacity to meet the unexpected with joy honors who we are as whole human beings.

AUTUMN —

FIRE

Delicious autumn! My very soul is wedded to it, and if I were a bird I would fly above the earth seeking successive autumns.

—George Eliot

OCTOBER

Goodbye and hello

A new baby, freshly born, has a monumental task ahead: getting to know the world. From the first breath, infants become embedded in the life around them. The rhythms of family life—waking and sleeping, eating and digesting, day and night—and the larger rhythms of nature's seasons provide a foundation that supports the child getting to know the world. The outer structure provided by parents supports the child in establishing healthy rhythms for going to sleep, experiencing hunger, eliminating, entering into times for play, going outside, being active and being still. In addition, parents also generally experience ease and health through these established rhythms.

The cyclical rhythm of the seasons offers much information to children on their journeys as they get to know the world. From birth onward, the child drinks in with the senses what is happening in the air and on the earth in nature. The infant can enter into this process of rhythm—for example, if held up to a window each morning as the parent says "good morning" to the new day. The toddler is able to experience and enter more actively into a relationship with the seasons. Parents and caregivers can encourage this relationship by taking children on walks in the forest and meadows, dancing in warm rain together, or greeting the sun each day with a cheery "Hello, sun!"

The children begin to observe that the earth is frozen and covered with snow, then delicate green shoots push through, next flowers and fruit, until the golden leaves sail through the air and the cycle begins again. During walks outside in nature, children form an active connection with the earth by gathering treasures—tiny pebbles, large stones, pinecones, acorns, flowers, bugs, bits of broken egg shells, and sometimes even a frog or two. Children often want to bring home many of these objects. What to do with them? There is a solution—a seasonal nature table.

Creating such a space, where the objects of nature are honored and their beauty appreciated, provides children with opportunities each day to learn reverence and gratitude. Especially at this time of year when the days are growing shorter and the dark darker, a nature table can bring warmth and joy into the home.

A seasonal nature table

Here are some tips for creating a place where the treasures of nature can coalesce into a scene inside your home. Updating the nature table regularly helps it to reflect what is happening outside.

First, choose a place for your nature table. This can be a small table, a shelf, the top of a piano, or a wide windowsill. It could be on a large tray, which makes it portable.

Some of the child's precious treasures gathered on walks can find a home on the nature table. In addition, parents can add other objects and gifts of nature to enhance the tableau. At this time of year, branches of beech and pine boughs may be added. It is all a matter of one's own connection with the seasons and personal creativity. Each family can choose whether the space is interactive or "for eyes only."

At bedtime, the rhythm of day and night can be honored as parents hold the young child up to a window and reverently say goodbye to the day and hello to Lady Moon.

In the rhythm of Autumn's return to New England, tons of leaves that were lifted up to treetops in the spring now lie on the forest floor, and children jump into parent-raked piles, scattering the leaves. Squirrels and chipmunks, with cheeks expanded to their limits, scurry back and forth, filling their winter homes with acorns and seeds. Beavers are cutting aspen trees and hauling them to their underwater dens for January dinners.

It is a time for getting ready for what is to come. Adults are hopefully having their chimneys cleaned, stacking cordwood, making sure there is a usable snow shovel, and getting in a good supply of candles.

As October progresses the evenings suddenly seem darker, the daylight comes later and the morning dew on the grass turns to frost; winter is approaching. We are once again reminded that our lives are not separate from the movements of the stars and planets. In ancient times human beings felt themselves directly connected with the celestial movements as well as deeply attuned to the rhythms of birth and death. They marked these changes of seasons and life rhythms with festivals of reverence and celebration.

The remnants of one of these festivals can be found in Halloween as it is celebrated today. One ancient festival, which originated with the early Celtic peoples, was celebrated on November 1 as a festival for the Celtic Sun God. This New Year's Day honored the sun and marked the beginning of winter. The sun, as ripener of the grain, was thanked for the harvest and offered strength for the coming battle with cold and dark. In anticipation of the coming darkness, bonfires were lit. These Celtic peoples believed that the souls of the departed were drawn by the fire to the warmth and light they remembered from former lives. They thought that all manner of ghosts, fairies, and hobgoblins walked abroad at this time of year. They believed that the fires would protect the people as well as appease the mischievous spirits. Thus, the festival was also celebrated to honor Samhain, the Lord of the Dead.

In later centuries this festival was recognized by the medieval European church and continued to be celebrated in honor of the transition from autumn to winter and to birth and death. The respect for and fear of the supernatural, invisible world and the realm of death remained strong. The people anticipated that ghosts, witches, and magic would abound on the night of October 31. They believed that disguising themselves as somebody else would protect them and their homes from any evil spirits that would come. It was also an evening to predict the future, as it was believed the intuitive forces were very strong on that night.

In the north of England, a bowl of porridge was set outside the door to appease any visiting spirits. To frighten away witches the people carved faces on hollowed out turnips and placed candles inside. Even though today fear has subsided, the elements of the festival have remained in playful fashion with dressing up, apple bobbing, and fortune telling with apple seeds and nuts. And of course, turning pumpkins into Jack-o-Lanterns and handing out treats to any visitors who come to your door on Halloween night.

How to bring Halloween to the young child?

It is important in bringing this festival to young children that both the spirit of the origin of Halloween as well as their developmental stage be honored. This age asks for goodness, beauty, and protection. For the children it is also a time of expanding imagination and constant transformation. To dress up means to change one's identity. Young children striving towards their own identity need to seek to identify with those worthy of imitation. They need to be able to become a character who represents a virtuous quality—beauty, goodness, courage, hard work, love, care for others, care for the earth.

Five- and six-year-olds can be guided to choose to be bakers, carpenters, sea captains, kings, queens, bee-keepers, farmers, doctors, nurses, mothers, knights, fishermen, pilots.

Three-and-four-year-olds are strongly connected to nature and can choose to be flower fairies, gnomes, kittens, bunnies, or lady bugs.

Little ones who travel with older siblings can be pumpkins, bees, or in a backpack with a gnome hat. Or they can be at home helping to pass out treats.

If you have time to help your child make a costume, what a wonderful gift. They can experience taking simple raw materials, perhaps even some well-used, recycled garment and a stick from the woods and transforming them into something beautiful, imaginative and fun. This is a way we can educate the children when they are young about being human. We show them that by making things with our hands, human beings have the power to transform nature. This is not only about making a Halloween costume; this is a gift for their whole lives.

> *Overalls, plaid shirt, straw hat and rake*
> *And a sheaf of straw, do a farmer make.*
> *White hat and mixing bowl, a pan for a cake*
> *Wooden spoon and apron do a baker make.*
> *Long pants and basket, then off to the lake,*
> *Long pole and line do a fisherman make.*

October is a bittersweet month. The joys of summer have receded in our memories, the once colorful landscapes have turned to rust and brown, our bodies are encumbered by jackets and hats. Yet there is the exciting possibility that life will become simpler. No more gardens to weed, no more lawns to mow, no more pickles to make. No more sand in the bathtub. Hiking on open trails in the clear, sparkling, bug-free air. The crisp air, clarity in our thinking, and then there is always the hope for snow.

NOVEMBER

Lighting the Way

Crisp, clear November days announce that a transition has occurred. Gone are the long, warm, lazy days of summer; even the warm afternoons of October have disappeared. Now mornings are frosty and late afternoons are cool. The light is sharper, the shadows deeper.

Something in the outer world has shifted whether we are aware or not. Nature no longer offers the same solace, excitement, and wonder that it did in June and July. Big questions about life begin to stir. Do I need to make a change of direction in my life? Who do I want to be? Am I happy with what I am doing? Where is my soul connected? Where is my spirit grounded? I have frequently asked these questions of myself. One would think that after many years these questions would be resolved. However, that is not the case. Like the horses on a carousel, they come around again each year, offering the rider another chance to catch the brass ring.

At the same time, outer situations, either of a personal or global nature, heap challenges upon us. Feelings of sadness, overwhelm, exhaustion, and hopelessness may begin to creep in. As the daylight diminishes, in the dark and growing shadows life may seem depressing, hopeless, challenges insurmountable. However, if we can hold on to our trust that the light will return our perspective can shift. If we address these feelings of sadness and concern, we can begin our journey inward to seek the light.

For children, there are festivals with images that portray going bravely into the dark as they journey toward the light. Against the backdrop of Michaelmas in September, they travel through the fall celebrations, their images portraying the increase of the light, giving the children a picture of hope and courage. Now in November, children have already experienced the lighted faces of golden pumpkins, going safely through the dark night to return home. Later might come a Lantern Walk, a walk in the dark carrying a lighted lantern—a light celebrating the love and care offered by a kind soldier named Martin, who cut his warm, woolen cloak in two and gave half to a beggar. This festival at night can become an image of compassion, which will later guide them for their future. How wonderful that children can be taken into the dark night in the presence of their trusted, loving caretakers.

Soon comes the Harvest Festival. Thanksgiving arrives with yellow squash, burgundy beets, orange pumpkins, and sheaves of golden grain. The bounty of the harvest is celebrated with family and friends in a glow of warmth and gratitude. People come together to share what they have prepared for the harvest meal. The earth has provided for us, and we are thankful. Human beings break bread together; a community is formed. A community we can call on as we proceed through the dark.

Thanksgiving is followed a few days later by the beginning of Advent, a time of intensification of the search for the light. Advent is a time of waiting. It is a period of four weeks of quiet when something new is being prepared. We must patiently wait for its arrival. However, this period of waiting is not about sitting back to see what comes. It asks that we are actively searching and preparing ourselves to be worthy of the gift.

Whatever your personal beliefs, there is the reality that in this month of waiting, the air is filled with a longing for the light. In the northern hemisphere, the light will begin to increase at the Solstice for everyone, whatever their beliefs, however they shape their journey through life. Even though we know that the sun will return, the days will grow longer, and the darkness will recede, still there can be a restlessness, a disturbance of the calm, quiet mood. We are called upon to actively work to find peace and hope within the outer and inner disturbances.

During this time of waiting, of preparing for the return of the light, as parents we are called upon also to bring to our children quiet, peaceful moments so they too can savor what can be found in the dark. Even though the stars cannot be seen in the day and the lighted lantern loses its magic in the light of the sun, still we trust that the stars exist and the lantern glows. We quietly wait as we sit with them in the peace that comes with silence, in the magic of sitting before one lighted candle. In community with our children, our families, our friends, we are given the opportunity to find our own way through the dark and into the light of hope, peace, and love.

After the dark days of late November, the promise of the sun's rebirth offers hope and joy. The birth of each child is also such a moment for hope and joy. Your child came down to earth from the heavenly realms as well. You know the facts of their journey and birth, but can you imagine, just for a moment, your child floating to earth holding the string of a red balloon?

You joyfully receive the child, red balloon and all. Then, as caregivers, it is your task to ensure that the balloon deflates gradually until your child can live on the earth as an independent adult. Rather than puncture the balloon to expedite the process, and perhaps precipitate a crash landing, it is important to support your child in touching down slowly and carefully. As we care for children through their first months and years, the challenge is how to protect and provide for them in ways that support healthy growth without artificially accelerating the process of incarnating, of coming to be on the earth as a human being.

How to do this? In the beginning, let them sleep, and sleep, and sleep. After all, they have arrived out of the womb where it was warm and cozy, nourishment was provided, and they floated in a watery sea that protected them from bumps and jostles. As a transition, let them sleep in a darkened room, perhaps even with a silk or delicate cloth over the crib. When not asleep, they lie in a dreamy haze; in the early weeks, eyes do not even focus. Let them come slowly into the light of day.

Then begins for you as a parent a time of making decisions for your children's well-being in the early years: what clothing, what activities, what environment. One way to provide this protection and care is to surround the very young children with objects and materials that are similar to the qualities they experienced in the womb—warm, cozy, life-giving. What a gift to offer the children toys made from substances that mirror the organic, alive qualities of the materials used. Toys made of wood are warm and welcoming. In wooden toys are hidden the compressed sunlight of years of growth in the light, as well as the hidden life forces from the dark earth. Natural fibers feel soft and warm and retain something of the qualities inherent in the original material. Clothing made from natural fibers holds an echo of something once alive, similar to the life that is now burgeoning in the child. After all, wool keeps the sheep warm in winter cold, so why not your child? Soft, over-all colors in clothing and walls allow the air to be slowly released from the "balloon" that carried your child to earth.

Late November activities to do with your children

Go out at night and say hello to the stars and the moon.

Pause at dinner or bedtime and quietly spend a few moments treasuring the glow of a lighted candle in the dark.

Move more slowly; savor the moments.

Without explanation, bring images, stories, songs of the light of the human spirit with its possibilities for love, caring, compassion.

Practical preparations for the winter holidays

In preparation for the approaching winter holidays, thoughts may be turning towards gifts for your children. In addition, grandparents, aunts, and uncles may be asking for gift suggestions. If you offer ideas, you may be able to steer family members to give the presents you would like for your children—objects that are made of natural materials, are beautiful, stand up to wear and tear, and are age-appropriate. In addition to toys, warm clothing made of natural fibers is always a bonus in New England!

Toy suggestions for each age

Following is a list of some toy suggestions suitable for the ages and stages of development of your young children.

Age One to Three

- Large knotted doll
- Soft balls for inside, rubber for outside
- Simple doll carriage
- Small wooden cart or wagon for inside
- Wagon for outdoors
- Basket of blocks of different shapes
- Rocking horse
- Wooden scoops
- Rocking board
- Pound-a-peg
- Small broom
- Sturdy scoop—plastic or metal for sandbox
- Boxes or baskets that nest like Russian nesting dolls
- Simple nesting dolls
- Wooden bowl and small wooden spoons for kitchen play
- Play silks
- Sheepskin
- Books with moveable pictures
- Rigid wire frame with sliding beads
- A small scoot ride-on toy for inside
- An inside swing if that works in the house

Age Three to Four

- Large pieces of solid color natural fabric for house building
- Play stands
- Large wooden clips
- Finger knitted cords
- Doll bed—can be a basket or simple wooden bed
- Baskets of all sizes
- China tea set
- Wooden top
- Doll—perhaps a heavy, weighted doll
- Moveable toys—chickens pecking on a board, two lumberjacks sawing
- Child sized real tools—broom, mop, shovel, rake
- Bubble bath
- Block crayons

Age Five to Seven

- More formed doll
- Doll clothes
- Stand-up puppets
- Project basket with "stuff" for making things—paper, paper punch, yarn, lots of masking tape, scotch tape, glue, etc.
- Sewing basket with pin cushion, needles, needle case, thimble, fabric, thread, yarn, embroidery hoop, scissors
- Basket of clothes pins or large clips for house building
- Large wagon
- Jump rope
- Beeswax for modeling
- Stick crayons (Stockmar brand or similar)

DECEMBER

Peaceful Moments

December brings the shortest, darkest days of the year. The sensation that the night is swallowing the day strengthens. For the young child, the day closes early, as the sun has already descended by dinnertime. A sense of quiet can be felt, unlike in the summer when the sun is still shining as the child goes to bed. Without choice, their physical bodies respond, usually with periods of longer and deeper sleep. One can sense they are being called out into the long, dark nights to commune with the stars.

In fact, in these mid-winter nights, the sleep of the young child is often deeper than at other times of the year. Parents can help guide the child into these nights of deep and restful sleep by creating a quiet mood at bedtime with gentle lullabies, a simple story, and a lighted candle. The glow of candlelight fills the room with a sense of peace and calm, preparing the child to enter this place of deep rest.

For parents, this may not be the case. Much may be on your minds after the relaxed days of summer. Dawn comes later, dusk earlier. Who would not like at this point in the year to curl up with the bears and squirrels in a snow cave or nest and hibernate until spring? But for caregivers, hibernation is not an option. Tummies continue to get hungry and diapers need to be changed. Yet inwardly there may remain the longing deep within you, as with the children, to commune with the stars.

Here in New England, life can add to the heaviness as it presents more challenges—wood to carry, snow to shovel, more time needed to layer the children in warm clothing, less sunshine each day to lift spirits. As well, there may be inner struggles arising from sudden illness, accidents, relationship challenges, or even the added stress of preparing for family celebrations. Parents are asked to stretch to encompass world events and catastrophes as well as the daily responsibilities of parenting.

Perhaps even before the child is asleep, the parents are thinking about all the extra tasks this time of year asks of them—getting ready for winter, holiday planning and preparation—activities that can leave the parents of young children doubly stretched, stressed, harried, and exhausted. Parents also need the nourishment of the calm and peace emanating from the lighted candles and quiet singing.

As December days progress, the outer darkness grows, eating the light one minute each morning and nibbling away again in the evening. In our souls this encroaching darkness can arouse dark thoughts and feelings—fear, anger, overwhelm, hopelessness, grief, sorrow, contraction. At the same time the outer world is bombarding us with an expanding energy that seems out of control. This swirling energy surrounds us whether we are part of it or not. Lists, shopping, presents, cards, concerts, and the invasion of advertising fill the air.

There is a background buzz that is hard to ignore.

In addition, there are the demands that we, as adults, put on ourselves; this shopping to complete, these cookies to bake, these presents to wrap, these solstice celebrations to prepare. Whatever traditions you may have, they easily contribute to more tasks to complete, less sleep, and more stress.

Yet if we can pause, we may hear something else. We may hear a whisper that asks us to slow down and listen. Whether it is a small voice calling from deep within, a message we receive in a holiday card, a song, or a niggling thought that won't go away, it streams into our consciousness. Whatever it is, something is calling us back to ourselves, to what is essential. In our hearts we all long for that which is so deeply human: peace and love.

The outer light will return, but it is the work of each individual to seek the inner light—to pay heed to the whisper which calls us back to our essential goodness. The returning outer light is a gift but the inner light we must find for ourselves. In our search, the universe offers us a reminder each evening as we look out into the dark night and see the stars.

While your mind is perhaps twirling, what your young children need from you at this busy season of the year is a sense of calm and steady peace, a mood that they can sink into and relax. Once you find this calm, peaceful place within yourselves, the children will be bathed in it. Like the colored liquid ascending the celery stalk in your seventh-grade science osmosis experiment, your children will drink in your inner mood of quiet and peace.

While we are pondering, and hopefully, simplifying, the young children are taking in, like a thirsty sponge, everything in their surroundings. It is our responsibility as caregivers to surround them with life-giving experiences, modeling for them the peace and love we want them to drink into their souls and eventually offer to others.

Peace

At this time of year especially, simplicity and candlelight go a long way in bringing times of calm and quiet into the home. Five minutes spent watching a candle glow, singing a seasonal song, and reminding oneself of what is essential is often enough to soothe a weary child or parent.

As busy parents of young children there may also be moments to savor that peace for ourselves, perhaps to sit in silence watching the candle's glow rather than mentally writing a shopping list.

Look at the list of tasks you want to accomplish this month and see them as *requests* of yourself as opposed to *demands* that you are required to complete. After all, you are in charge; you can cross items off without any fear that someone else will fire you. You are the boss.

Make a request of yourself that will nourish you. Take a walk outside in nature for ten minutes each day, spend five minutes reading something inspirational, sing while you work. The request you make of yourself for December days does not need to be big and complicated. A seemingly small deed when repeated daily can become a big contribution to your well-being. Your children will benefit from your efforts even if they are unaware of the intention you set for yourself. In the pause, you may even be able to hear the deep whisper.

Strive to model peace in your interactions. In resolving sibling conflicts, go slowly. Don't rush in to fix; listen to what each has to say about the "alleged transgressions." Listening will go a long way to resolving the conflict. The sense of being heard is a precious gift we give to our children.

Be gentle with yourself. Nobody but you will know what things you crossed off your list, nobody but you will know the knitted hat did not turn out exactly as you intended. Take a long soaking bath, turn on the radio and dance, eat a piece of chocolate.

Love

Involve your child in thinking about and making something to give to another. Bake cookies with them to share with neighbors or the elderly, let them put coins into the red buckets of the bell-ringers, make cards for grandparents. Even the youngest can glue and paste.

Take time out from busy, hectic days to offer extra hugs and lap time.

If you get frazzled, remember to breathe.

Find your kind words. Aloud, not necessarily directly to your child, express gratitude for the bounty that you have been given.

Be gentle and love yourself. Remember, not one of us is perfect.

Making space for a peaceful moment

If all these suggestions seem overwhelming, just light a candle; at the breakfast nook, even if you are hurrying to get everyone out the door, at the dinner table, as you put your child to bed. As you sit with your children, take in the glow in the room, in your children's faces as they drift off to sleep.

Perhaps even take a few minutes before you go to bed to sit quietly by yourself in the light of one candle.

Into deep darkness shines a light.
A candle flame burns clear and bright.

Amazing—the power of one light in the darkness to heal and bring peace.

May you and your family find peace and love in these coming weeks.

Growing as a Parent and a Person

Becoming a parent immediately sets us on a journey without a road map. We may not even have a clear picture of our destination. We rely on a mixture of books we have read, suggestions from grandparents and friends, the ways we were parented, and our own ideas and beliefs in order to make decisions, rerouting along the way as our children present us with ever-changing realities.

This task is even more challenging than it appears at first. Not only are we called upon to parent our children, we also have the responsibility to continue to be a parent to ourselves on our own journey through life, to care for who we are as an evolving human being, ever growing, ever changing. At the same time as we are strong for our children, we need to be strong for ourselves.

What is strong? Strong is not about having big biceps and tight abs. It is being healthy, centered, able to go through your days with minimal stress and overwhelm, to meet with equanimity what life presents to you each moment. It is OK and necessary to take care of yourself even as you are caring for your children. Not only is it OK, it is essential.If you are exhausted and have lost your sense of self, you will not be able to parent in the ways you would like. Look for ways to fill yourself up. An empty cup can offer no water to you or your children. It is necessary to replenish yourself so you can be present for your children.

Becoming a parent of children does not free one from continuing on a personal journey. We do not want to wake up one day to find ourselves sagging and limp, lost in a cloud of dust from washing dishes, changing diapers, folding laundry, cooking endless meals, and picking up a trail of cast-off clothing, soggy O-shaped cereal, and scattered toys.

The challenge arises—how do I do both? How do I parent myself at the same time I am parenting my children? Most parents may not realize they have probably heard an answer to that question multiple times in their lives. "Please fasten your seatbelt. In case of an emergency, put on your own oxygen mask first before you do so for your children." How simple yet how true. If you want to be strong for your children, you need to make sure that you are strong.

Self-care for the caregiver

Self-care often refers to caring for our bodies—healthy eating, caring for our skin, exercise. As caregivers, we wear many hats: cook, launderer, nurse, counselor, teacher, conflict mediator, psychic, athlete, magician, and a calm, centered presence, to name some. Wearing all these hats makes for a heavy load. A strong person is needed to fill these many roles, often several at the same time. It is necessary to attend to our diet, exercise, and health for our energy and well-being. It is also important to care for our bodies, as our bodies are where our souls and spirits reside.

What is self-care for the soul? For me, it means caring for my heart. Most important for me is to answer honestly the questions "What am I feeling?" "Am I finding in my life the qualities that I value and treasure, including honesty, choice, creativity, appreciation, respect, cooperation, support, being seen, being heard, and most basic of all, love?" "Is there any place in my life where I need to make amends?" If these values are met and the questions resolved, I can feel peaceful. I want to emphasize here that these values are not unique to me. In my cosmology all human beings value the same qualities that I do even if their actions say otherwise.

For me this means making sure my relationships are loving and respectful, staying connected with those closest to my heart, tending to unresolved situations that drain energy, sharing what I can offer with others. I strive to remind myself that I want to make choices based on what is good, what is true, what is beautiful. Is there beauty and clarity in this decision? Was I kind, or did I judge and criticize? Could I have been more compassionate? What can I do that will help me understand why she made that choice? I long to feel peace in my life of feelings.

Self-care for the spirit is another matter. Self-care for the body and soul have universal elements, while self-care for the spirit is totally individual. When children say "I" for the first time, around the age of three, they are announcing to themselves, you, and the world that they are unique individuals. Each child, each human being, is the only one who can use that word. We cannot use the word "I" and refer to another person. What power!

That "I" is our own spirit, our essential being, our uniqueness. Around the age of three it announces its arrival. It is then up to us to continue nourishing that "I" as we travel through life. So, in matters of the spirit, each of us is the only one who can make choices in regard to our spirit. Each of us must choose what offers truth, beauty and goodness to our spirit as our life unfolds. The discovery of what nourishes the deepest parts of our being is essential to our journey to personhood, to our path through life if we are to be happy, healthy, and whole. The nourishment may come through music, art, words, nature, people, solitude. Your "I" will recognize your source of renewal.

Just as our children are discovering the outside world, we have the opportunity to discover the world inside of us. Who am I? What is my life path? Are there habits and ways of thinking that I would like to transform? Enjoy discovering who you are!

Self-care for the body

• Choose foods that help your body feel good and healthy. Take time to care for your skin. Your skin embraces your whole body.

• Give yourself a foot massage with foot-care cream, while you say, "Thank you, feet, for carrying me through my days every step of the way."

• Dance while you stir the soup.

• Make time for activities that support your health and well-being. Yoga, Tai Chi, walking, hiking, swimming, massage, acupuncture, biking to name only a few.

• If you want, have some dark chocolate to balance all the chard and broccoli!

• BREATHE. Try in for a count of 4, out for a count of 8, for five minutes. It will lower your blood pressure.

Self-care for the soul

- Listen to your favorite music.

- Find a book you enjoy and keep it close by to pick up whenever you have a few free minutes.

- Invite a friend over for tea.

- Exchange childcare with another parent so you can occasionally have an hour to yourself.

- Keep a journal.

Choose an activity in which you can explore and express your creativity. This is not about creating a masterpiece. It is about bringing comfort to your soul. Knitting can be especially therapeutic; it offers focus, rhythm, and you have the pleasure of making something for yourself that you will enjoy, or a gift for someone else.

You may find while you are absorbed in what you are doing that your worries, concerns, and "to-do" lists disappear for a while and you can rest in the enjoyment of the moment. How restoring and refreshing! You are then ready to take up the responsibilities of caregiving again.

Take five minutes at the end of each day to reflect on how your day went. Look to see at what moments you would have liked taking a different action. Then with no self-judgment or criticism imagine how you might do it differently the next time a similar situation occurs. And no guilt! Judgment, criticism, blame, and guilt can tie up a tremendous amount of energy and resources. How wasteful! Instead of draining yourself, why not put this energy towards you and your family?

Look at what you enjoyed about the day and your actions. Where were truth, beauty, and goodness present and where were they missing? If you want to give yourself an extra challenge, go through your day backwards, in reverse.

After you have contemplated your own journey, you may decide to take on making a change in some aspect of your being. "I would like to form a new relationship with my sister." "I don't want to be so critical of my partner." Once you have a strategy and set out to make a change, don't worry if you frequently fail. It is the striving that is important. Your striving to transform yourself will have a profound effect on your children even if they have no understanding of the change you are attempting to make. What an amazing experience for a child: to witness people making changes in how they meet the world, transforming themselves.

Self-care for the spirit

• Choose an inspirational text for contemplation. Poetry, texts from all the world religions, and words from the sages are helpful places to begin. You need not choose an entire book or even a long passage. Much wisdom and guidance can be hidden in one sentence. Take five to ten minutes a day to read and contemplate the words you have selected.

• Set aside a time each day to restore and refresh yourself, even if it is only for five minutes.

• Pick up that old guitar or violin that you put in the closet many years ago.

• Take up an artistic activity that nourishes you. If you don't know what it might be, try several. It could also be as simple as taking up a pencil and a piece of blank paper and making a poem or sketch of the tree outside your window.

• Breathe!

Some of the above suggestions may support in more than one area. In the busy, speeded-up lives we seem to be living today, efficiency and conservation of energy are reasonable to consider. I have found several activities which support well-being for body, soul, and spirit for me. Three for the price of one!

• A long (at least 20 minutes) hot, soaking bath with Epsom salts and lavender oil soothes away the aches of body, soul, and spirit.

• A half-hour walk by myself. I get my heart rate up, my soul is soothed, and my spirit is lifted.

• Being outside in nature anywhere, anytime. Nature nourishes our senses, offers beauty to our souls, and fills our spirits with hope and joy!

I cannot emphasize enough how essential spending time outside in the natural world is to living a healthy life. Nature nourishes us, restores us, inspires us, heals us. The added benefit is that we can be outside, receiving all of the benefits that nature has to offer, at the same time we are with our children. Parenting ourselves while we parent our children; parenting our children while we parent ourselves!

Take care of yourself. Strive to be healthy in body, soul, and spirit. You owe it to yourself as well as your children! Remember, we shape our children's lives by how we live.

Fasten your seatbelt, put on your own oxygen mask, sit back, and enjoy the ride!

It's not only children who grow. Parents do, too. As much as we watch to see what our children do with their lives, they are watching us to see what we do with ours. I can't tell my children to reach for the sun. All I can do is reach for it, myself.

—Joyce Maynard, *Domestic Affairs*

In Gratitude

- To my children for being who you are. You have given me the possibility to experience unconditional love.

- To my grandmother, you taught me many truths about life, one being "If you are all dressed up, ready to go out, and your shoes aren't polished, the fancy dress is all for naught."

- To my father, who took me on long walks in the forest, hung up my beloved swing, and introduced me to gardening.

- To my mother, who offered me unconditional love even when I was a "wild child" of the 1960s. You taught me, "Don't be afraid to ask. The worst they can say is No." I heard your voice in my head as I emailed Susan Howard.

- To Susan Howard, you took me seriously when I approached you with my book idea. Without you it would not have happened.

- To Meggan Gill, you thoroughly polished my shoes. You helped me to clarify my intentions and often gave me words to describe the conundrum that was buzzing in my head. In you I found a companion on the journey of offering hope to this troubled world. I hope you enjoyed it as much as I did.

• To Lory Widmer Hess, you suggested a deadline which helped keep me on task. Your encouragement along the way was so supportive and you ironed out the wrinkles. Finally, you gave the shoes a second polishing, added the last bit of shine and saw that the shoes got to the dance.

• To all my colleagues at the High Mowing School over the last fifty years, you have nurtured and supported me in my journey as a teacher, colleague, and human being.

• To all the parents who have brought your children into my classes over these many years. You offered me trust and care; I learned many valuable lessons from you and your children.

• To Ann Pratt, who had the inspiration for the Pine Hill Waldorf School and saw potential in a long-haired, miniskirted Hippie.

• To my daughter, you willingly jumped in to join me in this endeavor even though it wasn't quite clear to either of us what I was asking. The drawings are wonderful and enhance the text. What fun to collaborate with you!

• To all the members of the Riverbank Writers, you have supported me in my writing since the group formed in 2020 and have offered much encouragement from the moment I first took up this book project.

About the Author

Sherry Jennings helped to found a Waldorf School in Wilton, New Hampshire, and together with her husband formed a Land Trust Community. There they built the house in which she continues to live after 45 years.

Sherry enjoys spending time with her three adult children and friends, reading, gardening, hiking, painting, writing, and spending time at her favorite beach in Maine. Themes which have carried her on her journey are the mystery of human connection and destiny.

About the Illustrator

Viorica Jennings resides in Los Angeles, California, where her lifelong love of creativity and nature continues to shape her work. She holds a minor in fine art and has spent many years supporting youth and families through various mental health and social service roles. These experiences deepen the empathy and imagination reflected in her illustrations.

When she is not creating art, Viorica enjoys spending time in the natural world, walking by the ocean, hiking, backpacking in the mountains, and being with her friends and family.

www.ingramcontent.com/pod-product-compliance
Lightning Source LLC
Chambersburg PA
CBHW061809070526
44586CB00024B/2768